India: The Investment Magnet

SANDEEP CHAVAN

Published by SANDEEP CHAVAN, 2024.

INDIA: THE INVESTMENT MAGNET

First edition. December 1, 2024.

ISBN: 979-8230440536

Written by SANDEEP CHAVAN.

Table of Contents

1. Introduction: India as the Investment Magnet 1
2. The Economic Magnet: India's Macro Landscape 10
3. The Technology Magnet: IT, Innovation, and Startups 21
4. The Manufacturing Magnet: Industry 4.0 and Beyond 33
5. The Green Magnet: Renewable Energy and Sustainability 46
6. The Healthcare Magnet: Pharmaceuticals and Biotech 59
7. The Infrastructure Magnet: Building the Future 73
8. The Agri-Tech Magnet: Revolutionizing Agriculture 88
9. The Consumer Magnet: India's Growing Middle Class 104
10. Overcoming Challenges: Navigating India's Investment Landscape 119
11. Real Stories: India's Investment Success Stories 132
12. Future Magnetism: What Lies Ahead for India 148
13. Practical Guide for Investors: How to Invest in India 165
14. Investment Opportunities in India's Stock Market 178
15. Conclusion: Seizing the Magnetic Opportunities in India 205
Appendices 214
Resources 218
Acknowledgments 221
About the Author 223

To the global investors who see beyond borders,Who recognize the potential of a billion aspirations,And who believe in the transformative power of innovation and growth—

This book is dedicated to you.

May it serve as a guiding light to navigate India's dynamic landscape,Inspire confidence to invest in its boundless opportunities,And empower you to contribute to a journey of progress that shapes not just a nation, but the world.

Your vision and actions are integral to realizing India's promise as a global economic powerhouse.

"The future belongs to those who see opportunities where others see challenges,and India is a land where opportunities abound."— Inspired by India's growth story

Disclaimer

The content of this book, **"India: The Investment Magnet – Opportunities across Key Sectors for Local and Global Investors,"** is for informational and educational purposes only. It is intended to provide general insights into India's economic landscape, key sectors, and investment opportunities. The information presented in this book is based on research, publicly available data, and the author's personal understanding and observations.

The author, **Sandeep Chavan**, is not a SEBI-registered investment advisor or financial professional. Any suggestions regarding specific companies, sectors, or investment opportunities are illustrative and should not be construed as financial advice, stock recommendations, or endorsements. Readers are encouraged to conduct their own due diligence and consult with certified financial advisors, investment professionals, or legal experts before making any financial decisions or investments.

The financial markets, regulatory frameworks, and economic conditions in India are dynamic and subject to change. While every effort has been made to ensure the accuracy and relevance of the information at the time of publication, the author and publisher cannot be held liable for any inaccuracies, omissions, or losses incurred based on the information provided in this book.

Investments in the stock market, equities, bonds, and other financial instruments carry inherent risks, including the loss of principal. Readers should carefully assess their financial situation, risk tolerance, and investment objectives before making any investment decisions.

This book is intended as a resource to provide a deeper understanding of India's investment ecosystem and does not serve as a substitute for professional financial advice. By using the information in this book, readers acknowledge and agree that the author and publisher are not responsible for the financial outcomes of their decisions.

Thank you for understanding the intent of this book, which is to empower, inform, and inspire investors to explore India's dynamic growth story responsibly and strategically.

Preface

India: The Investment Magnet – Opportunities across Key Sectors for Local and Global Investors is a journey into the heart of one of the most dynamic and transformative economies in the world. Over the past few decades, India has emerged as a land of unparalleled potential, combining the energy of a youthful population, the innovation of a thriving startup ecosystem, and the resilience of a diverse economic base. This book is an exploration of that journey, designed to empower investors, entrepreneurs, and leaders to unlock the opportunities within India's vibrant markets.

The idea for this book was born from my observation of India's remarkable trajectory—from a nation overcoming challenges of the past to one shaping the future of global commerce and innovation. As an engineer, educator, and lifelong observer of economic trends, I have witnessed firsthand the transformative power of strategic investments and forward-thinking policies. This book is my attempt to bring clarity to the complex yet rewarding landscape of investing in India.

India: The Investment Magnet provides a comprehensive overview of the sectors driving India's growth story, from its world-class IT industry and pharmaceutical leadership to its rising dominance in renewable energy, fintech, and agri-tech. It goes beyond the numbers to delve into the stories of companies and individuals who have embraced India's potential and thrived. From insights into government policies and investment frameworks to strategies for navigating challenges, this book serves as a practical guide for local and global investors alike.

The chapters are structured to provide readers with actionable insights into India's strengths, opportunities, and future trajectory. Whether you are an institutional investor exploring new markets, an entrepreneur seeking inspiration, or a policymaker looking for collaborative avenues, this book offers perspectives that are both informative and inspiring.

This book is not just about investment opportunities—it is about the people, ideas, and vision that make India the magnet it is today. It is an invitation to be part of a transformative journey, to contribute to India's growth story while reaping the rewards of its dynamic economy.

I dedicate this book to all those who believe in the power of opportunity and innovation, and to those who see India not just as a destination, but as a partner in shaping the future. I hope this book serves as a valuable resource for your endeavors and a testament to the boundless possibilities that India offers.

Thank you for joining me on this journey.

Sincerely,

Sandeep Chavan

1. Introduction: India as the Investment Magnet

"India: Where Innovation Meets Opportunity"

India stands at the crossroads of global economic dynamics, emerging as a magnet for investments both local and international. In a world seeking growth amid uncertainty, India shines as a stable, rapidly growing economy poised to shape the future of global markets.

With a vibrant economy, a burgeoning population, and a rapidly transforming business environment, the country presents a unique blend of opportunities that cater to a wide range of industries and investors. From its technological prowess driving the world's third-largest startup ecosystem to its strategic initiatives like *Make in India* and *Digital India*, India's appeal is both undeniable and unparalleled.

This chapter explores India's ascent as a global investment hub, highlighting why it has become a hotspot for innovation, manufacturing, and consumer-driven growth. It uncovers the reasons behind its magnetic pull for investors and the key achievements that solidify its position as a force to reckon with on the world stage.

Overview of India's Emergence as a Global Investment Hub

India's evolution into a global investment magnet is a testament to its resilience, adaptability, and ability to capitalize on opportunities in an ever-changing world. Over the past two decades, India has rewritten its economic narrative, moving from a predominantly agrarian base to becoming a diverse powerhouse that thrives on technology, manufacturing, and services. This transformation is no accident—it is the result of carefully orchestrated strategies, forward-thinking policies, and a relentless focus on innovation.

At the heart of this journey lies India's ability to leverage its traditional strengths while embracing modern capabilities. It is a land where the ancient ethos of entrepreneurship intersects with cutting-edge technology, creating an environment ripe for growth and investment. No longer just a destination for low-cost labor or outsourcing, India today is a thriving hub of innovation, known for its vibrant startup ecosystem and robust industrial infrastructure.

Strategic Reforms Driving the Transformation

The structural reforms implemented over the years have acted as the bedrock of India's economic ascent. Policies such as the introduction of the Goods and Services Tax (GST), the Insolvency and Bankruptcy Code (IBC), and labor law reforms have streamlined business operations, making it easier for companies to establish and expand their presence in India. These changes have not only improved India's ease of doing business rankings but also attracted global investors seeking stability and predictability in their investments.

Infrastructure development has been another key pillar in India's growth story. Mega projects like the Bharatmala road network, Sagarmala port development, and the Delhi-Mumbai Industrial Corridor have enhanced connectivity, reduced logistics costs, and boosted industrial activity. These initiatives signal to investors that India is not only open for business but is actively building the frameworks necessary to support sustained economic growth.

A Laboratory for Innovation

India's appeal goes beyond being just a market; it has evolved into a laboratory for innovation. The sheer scale and diversity of its population present unparalleled opportunities for companies to test, refine, and scale their products. From mobile payment solutions that cater to millions of unbanked citizens to electric vehicles tailored for urban congestion, India provides fertile ground for groundbreaking ideas to take root and flourish.

Initiatives like *Make in India*, *Digital India*, and *Startup India* have further solidified its position as a preferred investment destination. Under the *Make in India* program, sectors such as electronics, defense, and renewable energy have witnessed a surge in domestic and international investments. *Digital India* has driven the penetration of technology across urban and rural areas, transforming India into one of the largest markets for digital services. Meanwhile, *Startup*

India has nurtured the growth of a dynamic startup ecosystem, producing over 100 unicorns and attracting venture capital from around the globe.

A Competitive Edge

What sets India apart is its ability to offer a comprehensive value proposition. It combines a massive consumer base with a competitive cost structure, supported by an ever-improving business environment. Its young and dynamic workforce, paired with a culture of entrepreneurship, ensures that businesses have the talent and drive needed to succeed. This competitive edge has drawn companies ranging from tech giants like Google and Microsoft to manufacturing leaders like Tesla and Foxconn to invest and expand in India.

India's emergence as a global investment hub is not just a story of growth; it is a story of transformation and ambition. By blending its rich heritage with futuristic policies and innovation, India has positioned itself as a beacon for investors worldwide. In the chapters to come, we will explore how India's diverse sectors and dynamic environment continue to attract and inspire investment, paving the way for a prosperous future.

Why Investors are Flocking to India

India's magnetic pull for investors lies in its compelling combination of demographics, market size, economic resilience, and technological advancements. As one of the fastest-growing major economies globally, India offers unmatched opportunities that cater to diverse industries and investor interests. Below are the key reasons why local and global investors are increasingly drawn to this dynamic nation.

Demographics: A Young and Dynamic Workforce

India's youthful demographic is one of its most significant assets, providing a distinct competitive advantage in the global marketplace. With a median age of around 28 years, India is home to one of the youngest workforces in the world, poised to drive innovation, productivity, and economic growth for decades to come.

Each year, over 10 million individuals enter the workforce, contributing to a talent pool that is not only vast but also increasingly skilled in emerging areas such as information technology, artificial intelligence, and renewable energy.

India's focus on education and skill development, exemplified by initiatives like the Skill India Mission, ensures that its workforce remains ready to meet the demands of modern industries.

For investors, this young and dynamic labor force translates into cost-effective operations, a readiness to adopt new technologies, and the human capital necessary to build and sustain cutting-edge enterprises across sectors like IT, manufacturing, healthcare, and services.

Market Size: The Consumer Magnet

India's population of over 1.4 billion represents one of the largest and most diverse consumer bases in the world. This sheer scale makes the country a magnet for businesses looking to tap into a market with virtually limitless potential.

The rising middle class is at the heart of this consumer-driven economy. By 2030, an estimated 70% of India's population will belong to this burgeoning middle class, which is driving demand across a wide range of sectors, including retail, real estate, healthcare, e-commerce, and education. This demographic shift is accompanied by increasing disposable incomes and urbanization, fueling a rapid expansion in consumer spending, which is expected to reach $8.6 trillion by 2030.

Global brands like Amazon, IKEA, and Apple have already recognized India's potential and are making significant inroads into the market. Simultaneously, homegrown startups and businesses are catering to the unique needs and preferences of Indian consumers, further enriching the ecosystem. For investors, India offers not just scale but also diversity, with opportunities to cater to urban and rural markets alike.

Economic Growth: A Resilient Trajectory

India's economy has consistently demonstrated resilience and adaptability, making it a reliable destination for investments even during global economic downturns. Over the past decade, India's GDP has grown at an average rate of 6-7%, with robust domestic consumption and a diversified economic base underpinning this growth.

Key structural reforms, such as the implementation of the Goods and Services Tax (GST) and the Insolvency and Bankruptcy Code (IBC), have streamlined business processes and bolstered investor confidence. Analysts predict that India will become the third-largest economy by 2030, further strengthening its position as a global economic powerhouse.

India's growth story is not limited to traditional sectors. Emerging industries such as renewable energy, electric vehicles, and advanced manufacturing are set to play a pivotal role in its economic trajectory. For investors, this resilience and diversity of opportunities provide a stable foundation for long-term returns.

Technological Advancements and Innovation

India has firmly established itself as a global leader in technology and innovation. Home to the world's third-largest startup ecosystem, India has nurtured over 100 unicorns as of 2024, spanning industries like fintech, edtech, healthtech, and agritech. These startups are not only revolutionizing domestic markets but are also making waves on the global stage.

The government's *Digital India* initiative has been a game-changer, driving the digital transformation of industries and creating a thriving ecosystem for tech investments. With one of the highest internet penetration rates globally and a population eager to adopt digital solutions, India offers unparalleled opportunities in e-commerce, fintech, and digital services.

Additionally, India's focus on research and development in emerging technologies such as artificial intelligence, blockchain, and quantum computing positions it as a hub for innovation. Global tech giants, including Google, Microsoft, and Amazon, continue to invest heavily in India, drawn by its talent pool and the potential for market expansion.

In conclusion, India's unique blend of demographic advantages, market size, economic resilience, and technological innovation creates an irresistible allure for investors. Whether it's the promise of a young and skilled workforce, the opportunity to cater to a vast and diverse consumer base, or the chance to participate in a rapidly evolving technological landscape, India offers something for every investor. As the chapters ahead will explore, these foundational strengths are complemented by sector-specific opportunities that further enhance India's position as the ultimate investment magnet.

A Snapshot of India's Achievements in Attracting Investments

India's meteoric rise as an investment magnet is a direct result of its strategic focus on policy reforms, infrastructure development, and technological innovation. The country's achievements across multiple domains highlight its commitment to fostering a business-friendly environment and positioning itself as a global economic powerhouse. Here is an expanded view of the milestones that underscore India's success in attracting investments:

Record FDI Inflows

India's ability to attract Foreign Direct Investment (FDI) has been a hallmark of its economic strategy. In 2023-24, the country received over $80 billion in FDI, a record high that underscores the global confidence in India's economic policies and growth potential.

Key drivers behind this success include liberalized FDI policies in sectors like defense, retail, and telecommunications, alongside targeted initiatives such as Production Linked Incentive (PLI) schemes. These measures have encouraged both global giants and domestic players to invest heavily in India, strengthening its position as a preferred destination for capital inflows.

Ease of Doing Business: Simplified and Streamlined

India's climb to the 63rd position in the World Bank's *Ease of Doing Business* rankings is a testament to its relentless pursuit of reform. Significant strides in taxation, licensing, and regulatory compliance have simplified processes for businesses, making it easier for investors to establish and operate their ventures.

The introduction of the Goods and Services Tax (GST) has unified India's complex tax system, reducing inefficiencies and creating a seamless business environment. Initiatives like single-window clearances for approvals and the digitization of government services further enhance transparency and reduce bureaucratic bottlenecks, making India an attractive proposition for investors.

Manufacturing Excellence: The Make in India Revolution

The *Make in India* initiative has been a game-changer for the country's manufacturing sector. By incentivizing production and fostering a culture of innovation, this program has attracted significant investments in industries like automotive, electronics, and renewable energy.

India has become a hub for electric vehicle (EV) manufacturing, with global leaders like Tesla and domestic champions like Tata Motors spearheading the shift towards sustainable mobility. In electronics, India has emerged as a key player, with companies such as Foxconn setting up large-scale manufacturing units to cater to both domestic and international markets. Renewable energy projects, driven by India's ambitious goals for solar and wind power, have also seen substantial foreign investment, solidifying the country's role in the green energy transition.

Infrastructure Development: Building for the Future

India's focus on infrastructure development has created a solid foundation for sustained economic growth and investment. Mega projects like the Delhi-Mumbai Industrial Corridor (DMIC) and Bharatmala Pariyojana exemplify the scale and ambition of India's infrastructure push.

Delhi-Mumbai Industrial Corridor (DMIC): A $100 billion initiative to create a world-class industrial zone, integrating smart cities, transport networks, and state-of-the-art logistics facilities.

Bharatmala Pariyojana: A nationwide project aimed at building 83,000 kilometers of highways, reducing logistics costs and enhancing regional connectivity.

Such initiatives not only improve the ease of doing business but also open up new avenues for investment in logistics, real estate, and allied industries.

Digital Economy Leadership: The Fintech and Payments Powerhouse

India's leadership in the digital economy is unparalleled, with its fintech sector valued at over $50 billion and projected to grow exponentially. The Unified Payments Interface (UPI), a revolutionary digital payments platform, processes over 10 billion transactions monthly, making India a global leader in cashless payments.

Programs like *Digital India* have accelerated the adoption of technology across urban and rural areas, transforming industries such as banking, e-commerce, and education. Global investors are flocking to this sector, recognizing the immense potential of India's digitally empowered economy. With innovations in artificial intelligence, blockchain, and data analytics, India is poised to remain at the forefront of the global digital transformation.

In summary, India's achievements in attracting investments reflect its commitment to fostering an inclusive, innovative, and investor-friendly ecosystem. From record-breaking FDI inflows to transformative infrastructure projects and digital advancements, India continues to position itself as a global leader in economic growth and development. These milestones not only attract investments but also reinforce India's narrative as a land of opportunities, ready to lead the charge in shaping the future of the global economy.

Conclusion

India's transformation into a global investment hub is a narrative of vision, perseverance, and adaptability. This remarkable journey is not an overnight phenomenon but the result of decades of sustained efforts in shaping a conducive business environment through strategic policy-making, robust infrastructure development, and a keen embrace of technological innovation. Each of these pillars has contributed to creating a foundation that continues to attract both local and global investors.

At the core of this success lies India's unique demographic advantage. With one of the youngest populations globally, the country offers an energetic, innovative, and adaptable workforce that fuels its industries and drives economic growth. Coupled with a vast and diverse market of over 1.4 billion people, India provides businesses with the rare opportunity to cater to both emerging urban centers and untapped rural segments.

Moreover, India's consistent economic growth underscores its resilience and adaptability in the face of global challenges. As one of the fastest-growing major economies, the country has maintained a trajectory that instills confidence among investors. Its ability to balance domestic consumption with export-oriented production ensures a diversified economic base that mitigates risks and enhances stability.

What sets India apart is not just its scale but the dynamism of its investment landscape. Programs like *Make in India*, *Digital India*, and *Startup*

India have amplified its appeal by fostering innovation, enhancing industrial capabilities, and promoting entrepreneurship. Mega infrastructure projects like the Delhi-Mumbai Industrial Corridor and Bharatmala Pariyojana are reshaping the logistical and operational framework of the nation, paving the way for seamless business operations. India's fintech revolution and digital economy leadership further highlight its forward-thinking approach to economic development.

Looking ahead, India's sectoral strengths—from technology and healthcare to renewable energy and manufacturing—offer investors a diverse array of opportunities. Each sector tells a story of growth, innovation, and the potential to make a significant global impact. India's commitment to sustainability, digital transformation, and inclusive growth positions it as the investment magnet of the 21st century, appealing to forward-thinking investors who value both profitability and purpose.

As subsequent chapters will delve deeper into these sectoral opportunities, they will reveal the rich tapestry of India's investment ecosystem and how it continues to evolve. Whether it's tapping into the vibrant startup scene, capitalizing on manufacturing excellence, or exploring the burgeoning green economy, India promises a future where investments are not only lucrative but transformative. The story of India is one of potential realized, and the opportunities it presents to investors are as boundless as its ambition.

India isn't just a destination for investments—it's a partner in shaping the global economy for the future. The chapters ahead will unpack these opportunities, offering a comprehensive guide for those ready to be part of this dynamic journey.

2. The Economic Magnet: India's Macro Landscape

"India: Where Opportunity Meets Resilience"

India's economic landscape is as diverse and dynamic as the nation itself, offering a rich tapestry of opportunities for investors across the globe. With its unparalleled growth trajectory and an ecosystem fueled by reform, innovation, and domestic consumption, India is redefining what it means to be a modern economic powerhouse.

As one of the fastest-growing major economies, India has consistently demonstrated resilience and adaptability, earning its place as a standout destination in the global investment arena. This chapter explores the country's robust economic fundamentals, the key drivers of its growth, and the transformative reforms that have redefined its investment ecosystem. It also sheds light on India's remarkable ability to weather global economic challenges, further solidifying its position as an indispensable partner in shaping the future of global commerce.

Insights into India's Economic Fundamentals

At the heart of India's magnetism for investors lies its robust and dynamic economic fundamentals. With a GDP exceeding $3.7 trillion in 2024, India stands as the world's fifth-largest economy and is on track to become the third-largest by 2030. This rapid growth trajectory is underpinned by a unique combination of strengths: a youthful workforce, a diversified economic base, and an ever-expanding domestic market. Together, these attributes create a foundation that is both resilient and ripe for investment opportunities across a spectrum of traditional and emerging industries.

Demographic Dividend: A Young and Energetic Workforce

India's population of over 1.4 billion is not just a vast consumer base but also a significant economic asset. With a median age of 28 years, India enjoys one of the youngest populations in the world, positioning itself as a global talent hub for decades to come.

This youthful demographic ensures a steady supply of labor across industries and fosters an environment of innovation and adaptability. Each year, millions of young Indians enter the workforce, contributing to sectors ranging from IT and manufacturing to services and agriculture. The government's *Skill India* initiative further enhances employability by bridging skill gaps and preparing the workforce for future demands in advanced industries like artificial intelligence, renewable energy, and healthcare.

For investors, India's demographic dividend translates into a cost-effective, highly adaptable labor pool that supports scalable business operations, making it an ideal destination for both labor-intensive and knowledge-driven industries.

Diverse Economic Base: A Balanced Growth Model

India's economy is a mosaic of diverse industries, providing opportunities across traditional sectors like agriculture as well as modern fields like IT and pharmaceuticals.

Agriculture: Despite rapid industrialization, agriculture remains a cornerstone of India's economy, supporting nearly half of its population. Recent innovations in agri-tech and government policies like *PM-Kisan* and *E-NAM* (National Agriculture Market) have modernized the sector, opening avenues for investment in smart farming, food processing, and export-oriented agribusiness.

Manufacturing: With initiatives like *Make in India*, the manufacturing sector is witnessing a renaissance, particularly in electronics, automotive, and aerospace industries. India is emerging as a global hub for electric vehicle (EV) production, supported by substantial investments from domestic giants and international players.

IT and Services: India is a global leader in IT services and outsourcing, contributing over 50% of its GDP. Cities like Bengaluru, Hyderabad, and Pune are hotspots for software development, fintech, and artificial intelligence research. The country's IT sector has consistently attracted global clients, delivering cost-effective, high-quality solutions.

The diversity of India's economic base not only drives growth but also ensures resilience against external shocks, offering a balanced and stable environment for investments.

Domestic Consumption as a Growth Driver: A Thriving Consumer Economy

India's economic growth is unique in its reliance on domestic consumption as a primary driver, making it less vulnerable to global trade fluctuations. The rising middle class, urbanization, and increasing disposable incomes have created a thriving consumer economy that continues to expand at an unprecedented pace.

Middle Class Revolution: By 2030, India's middle class is expected to account for 70% of its population, driving demand across sectors such as retail, real estate, healthcare, and e-commerce. The burgeoning middle class is not only spending more but also seeking quality and innovation, presenting opportunities for global brands and startups to tap into a discerning market.

Urbanization: India's urban population is projected to reach 600 million by 2030, fueling growth in infrastructure, housing, and public services. The demand for urban amenities has spurred investment in smart cities, public transport, and energy-efficient solutions.

E-commerce Boom: The digital revolution has transformed how Indians shop, with e-commerce platforms experiencing explosive growth. Companies like Flipkart, Amazon, and Nykaa are capitalizing on this trend, supported by logistics networks and digital payment systems like UPI.

For investors, this thriving consumer economy represents a vast and growing market with opportunities to cater to diverse preferences across urban and rural populations. Whether it's luxury goods or essential services, the potential for growth is immense.

In summary, India's economic fundamentals are a powerful magnet for investors, characterized by a youthful workforce, a diversified industrial base, and a consumer-driven growth model. These strengths not only drive India's rapid ascent as a global economic powerhouse but also provide a stable and scalable foundation for businesses. The combination of demographic dynamism, sectoral diversity, and robust domestic demand ensures that India remains a top destination for investment, offering unparalleled opportunities in the decades ahead. As we move further into the narrative, these fundamentals will serve as the bedrock for exploring India's sector-specific strengths and its role in shaping the global economy.

Key Growth Drivers and Reforms Shaping the Investment Ecosystem

India's growth story is no accident; it is the result of well-planned, deliberate efforts to create a business-friendly environment that attracts both domestic and international investors. The country's economic landscape has been reshaped through structural reforms, targeted incentive schemes, robust infrastructure development, digital transformation, and a flourishing startup ecosystem. These initiatives collectively enhance India's appeal as a global investment magnet.

Structural Reforms: Laying the Foundation for Growth

India's structural reforms have fundamentally altered the way businesses operate, making processes more transparent, efficient, and investor-friendly.

Goods and Services Tax (GST): The introduction of GST marked a paradigm shift in India's tax system. By unifying the country into a single market, GST has eliminated the complexities of multiple indirect taxes and reduced compliance burdens. Businesses now benefit from a simplified tax structure that fosters ease of operations and lowers logistics costs, making India more competitive on the global stage.

Insolvency and Bankruptcy Code (IBC): The IBC has strengthened India's financial ecosystem by providing a streamlined mechanism for resolving bad loans and insolvencies. It has increased creditor confidence and reduced the time taken to settle disputes, ensuring that businesses can recover and reallocate capital more effectively.

Labor Law Reforms: India has consolidated its numerous labor laws into four simplified codes, covering wages, industrial relations, social security, and occupational safety. These reforms provide greater flexibility in hiring and compliance, making India an attractive destination for industries requiring a large workforce.

Production Linked Incentive (PLI) Schemes: Boosting Manufacturing

The PLI schemes have emerged as a cornerstone of India's push to become a global manufacturing hub. These schemes provide financial incentives to domestic and foreign manufacturers across sectors like electronics, pharmaceuticals, renewable energy, and automotive.

Electronics and Technology: India has become a significant player in the global electronics supply chain, with PLI schemes attracting investments from companies like Foxconn, Samsung, and Apple. These initiatives aim to reduce import dependency while building a robust local ecosystem.

Renewable Energy: With its ambitious goals for solar and wind energy, India has leveraged PLI schemes to attract investments in battery storage, green hydrogen, and other renewable technologies.

The success of the PLI schemes underscores India's commitment to fostering industries that align with global trends and sustainability goals.

Infrastructure Development: Building the Backbone of Growth

Infrastructure development has been a top priority for India, as it directly impacts business efficiency and competitiveness. The government's ambitious projects are transforming the nation's logistical and industrial landscape:

Bharatmala Pariyojana: Aimed at improving road connectivity, this project involves the construction of over 83,000 kilometers of highways. It reduces logistics costs, enhances regional connectivity, and facilitates smoother movement of goods.

Sagarmala Program: Focused on port-led development, Sagarmala is transforming India's coastline into a driver of economic growth by enhancing port capacity, efficiency, and connectivity.

Delhi-Mumbai Industrial Corridor (DMIC): One of the world's most ambitious infrastructure projects, DMIC aims to create a high-tech industrial zone with world-class connectivity, smart cities, and integrated logistics.

These infrastructure initiatives are not only boosting industrial efficiency but also opening up new opportunities for investors in real estate, logistics, and allied industries.

Digital Transformation: Leading the Way in Innovation

India's digital revolution has been a game-changer for its economy, enabling seamless business operations and fostering a culture of transparency and accountability.

Unified Payments Interface (UPI): India leads the world in digital payments, with UPI processing over 10 billion transactions monthly. This widespread adoption of cashless transactions has revolutionized retail, e-commerce, and banking.

Digital Governance: Programs like *Digital India* have digitized essential government services, reducing red tape and enhancing accessibility for businesses and citizens alike. Online portals for tax filings, licenses, and approvals have significantly improved the ease of doing business.

Emerging Technologies: India is rapidly adopting technologies like artificial intelligence, blockchain, and IoT, creating opportunities for investment in tech-driven industries.

Startup Ecosystem: A Hotbed of Innovation

India's startup ecosystem is among the most vibrant in the world, with over 100 unicorns as of 2024 and counting. The *Startup India* initiative has played a pivotal role in nurturing entrepreneurial talent by offering funding support, tax exemptions, and simplified compliance procedures.

Funding and Mentorship: Access to venture capital and angel investors, combined with government-backed funds, has enabled startups to scale rapidly.

Sectoral Growth: Startups in fintech, edtech, healthtech, and agritech are revolutionizing their respective sectors, attracting investments from global players.

Global Collaborations: Indian startups are increasingly forming partnerships with international companies, integrating into global supply chains and markets.

The startup ecosystem showcases India's innovative spirit and its potential to drive technological advancements globally.

In conclusion, India's growth drivers and reforms have laid a strong foundation for an investor-friendly ecosystem. From structural reforms that streamline operations to incentive schemes that boost manufacturing, and from ambitious infrastructure projects to digital transformation and startup innovation, India offers a comprehensive and forward-looking environment for businesses. These initiatives not only enhance India's competitiveness but also reaffirm its position as a global investment magnet. As the journey continues, these reforms will play a pivotal role in shaping India's future as a leading economic powerhouse.

India's Resilience during Global Economic Challenges

India's ability to withstand global economic turbulence is a testament to its robust economic architecture and strategic adaptability. While the world grappled with the aftershocks of the COVID-19 pandemic, escalating trade wars, and rising geopolitical tensions, India emerged as a resilient force, leveraging its inherent strengths and proactive policy measures. This section explores how India has successfully navigated these challenges, setting a benchmark for economic stability in an increasingly volatile global landscape.

Self-Reliance through Atmanirbhar Bharat

Launched during the unprecedented disruptions of the COVID-19 pandemic, the *Atmanirbhar Bharat* (Self-Reliant India) initiative marked a transformative moment for India's economic strategy. This visionary policy framework aimed to reduce import dependency and bolster domestic production across critical sectors such as pharmaceuticals, defense, and manufacturing.

Pharmaceutical Independence: During the pandemic, India capitalized on its status as the "pharmacy of the world," ensuring a steady supply of essential medicines and vaccines, not just domestically but globally. The focus on self-reliance in pharmaceutical production has since expanded to Active Pharmaceutical Ingredients (APIs), reducing reliance on imports.

Defense Manufacturing: The initiative spurred a wave of domestic innovation in defense manufacturing, with programs encouraging partnerships between private companies and the government. Policies like raising the FDI limit in defense and earmarking defense procurement budgets for local suppliers have boosted the sector's self-sufficiency.

Atmanirbhar Bharat not only addressed immediate supply chain vulnerabilities but also laid the foundation for long-term economic resilience by promoting local industries and innovation.

Robust Domestic Consumption: The Backbone of Growth

Unlike many export-reliant economies that were severely impacted by disruptions in global trade, India's growth is largely underpinned by its strong domestic consumption. This intrinsic strength acted as a buffer against external shocks during crises.

Rising Middle Class: With a growing middle class accounting for a significant portion of the population, domestic consumption across sectors such as retail, real estate, and e-commerce remained robust even during global slowdowns.

Resilient Rural Economy: Government schemes like *PM-Kisan* and *Mahatma Gandhi National Rural Employment Guarantee Act (MGNREGA)* ensured continued financial support for rural households, sustaining demand for essential goods and services in rural India.

Digital Consumerism: The pandemic accelerated India's digital transformation, with e-commerce platforms, digital payments, and online services thriving despite economic uncertainties. This shift further bolstered domestic consumption and insulated the economy from global trade disruptions.

India's domestic market, with its scale and diversity, remains one of the most compelling factors for investors, providing stability during global economic turbulence.

Diversified Trade Partnerships: Spreading the Risk

India's engagement with multiple trade blocs and bilateral agreements has been instrumental in mitigating the risks associated with over-reliance on any single trading partner or region.

Act East Policy: Strengthening ties with Southeast Asian nations has expanded trade and investment opportunities in high-growth markets, reducing dependency on traditional partners.

Strategic Partnerships: Agreements with countries like the UAE, Japan, and Australia have diversified trade avenues, ensuring a steady flow of imports and exports even during global uncertainties.

Decoupling from Overreliance: India's cautious approach to aligning with major global powers has allowed it to maintain balanced trade relations. For instance, while engaging with the U.S. and Europe, India has also strengthened ties with emerging economies in Africa and Latin America, creating a multi-polar trade strategy.

This diversification strategy ensures that India's economy remains resilient and adaptive to shifts in global trade dynamics.

Stable Macroeconomic Policies: A Pillar of Confidence

India's ability to maintain macroeconomic stability during global crises has been a defining feature of its resilience. Key policies and measures have ensured that the economy remains robust and investor-friendly.

Fiscal Prudence: India's government has managed fiscal deficits strategically, balancing expenditure on growth-oriented projects with the need to maintain fiscal discipline. This prudent approach has helped sustain investor confidence during volatile periods.

Inflation Control: The Reserve Bank of India (RBI) has proactively managed inflation, ensuring that it remains within target ranges. This stability has been critical in maintaining purchasing power and supporting economic activities.

Proactive Monetary Policies: During the pandemic, the RBI implemented timely measures such as interest rate cuts, liquidity infusions, and moratoriums to support businesses and individuals. These measures cushioned the economic impact of the crisis and facilitated a faster recovery.

The combination of fiscal and monetary policies has positioned India as a stable and reliable economy, even amidst global uncertainties.

In conclusion, India's resilience during global economic challenges underscores its inherent strengths and strategic adaptability. From fostering self-reliance through initiatives like *Atmanirbhar Bharat* to leveraging its robust domestic market and diversifying trade partnerships, India has emerged as a model of economic stability. Its sound macroeconomic policies and ability to balance immediate needs with long-term goals have further solidified its position as a global investment magnet.

In a world marked by uncertainty, India's resilience not only assures investors of stability but also showcases the potential for sustained growth in the years to come. As we delve deeper into India's sectoral strengths in the following chapters, this foundation of resilience will serve as a recurring theme, highlighting why India continues to attract investments from across the globe.

Conclusion

India's macroeconomic landscape stands as a compelling testament to its emergence as a global investment magnet. Anchored in robust economic fundamentals, India's journey is shaped by deliberate policies, transformative reforms, and a commitment to fostering a business-friendly environment. The country's ability to navigate challenges and leverage its diverse strengths ensures a fertile ground for investments, setting it apart as a beacon of growth and opportunity.

The interplay of dynamic growth drivers and resilience has positioned India as a reliable and attractive destination for investors worldwide. The proactive approach to policy-making, from streamlining tax structures with GST to incentivizing domestic production through PLI schemes, has created an ecosystem where businesses can not only establish themselves but also flourish. Infrastructure development, digital transformation, and structural reforms further amplify this appeal, signaling a readiness to accommodate the demands of a globalized economy.

As a rapidly diversifying economy, India offers unmatched opportunities across traditional and emerging sectors. Its manufacturing capabilities, technology-driven advancements, and thriving startup ecosystem underscore its capacity for innovation, while a robust domestic market ensures a consistent demand base for businesses.

In the chapters ahead, we will explore India's sectoral strengths in greater detail, revealing how its multifaceted economy continues to evolve and adapt to global trends. From technology to renewable energy, and from healthcare to manufacturing, India's innovative spirit and sectoral depth promise a wealth of opportunities for investors seeking growth in an increasingly interconnected world. India's story is one of ambition and action—a nation embracing its potential as a global leader in shaping the future of business and investments.

3. The Technology Magnet: IT, Innovation, and Startups

"India: Where Technology Shapes Tomorrow"

India's technology sector stands as a cornerstone of its economic strength, celebrated globally for its unparalleled dynamism, innovation, and scale. From revolutionizing IT services to pioneering breakthroughs in emerging technologies, India has solidified its position as a magnet for technological investments worldwide. Its vibrant startup ecosystem, characterized by relentless creativity and entrepreneurial zeal, further propels the nation into the forefront of global innovation.

This chapter explores the evolution of India's IT industry as a global outsourcing powerhouse, its expanding influence in cutting-edge technologies such as AI and blockchain, and the remarkable growth of its startup ecosystem, which continues to drive transformative change and attract investments from across the globe.

India's IT Industry: The Global Outsourcing Powerhouse

India's IT industry stands as a beacon of excellence and a cornerstone of the nation's economic success. Renowned for its unparalleled proficiency in software services and global outsourcing, the sector has become synonymous with reliability, innovation, and scalability. Over the decades, this industry has grown into a key pillar of the Indian economy, contributing over 8% to the nation's GDP and employing more than 4.5 million professionals. Its evolution reflects a journey of consistent growth, adaptability, and a relentless pursuit of innovation.

Scale and Expertise: Dominating the Global IT Landscape

Indian IT companies like **Tata Consultancy Services (TCS)**, **Infosys**, and **Wipro** have carved a dominant position in the global IT services market. Their extensive networks span continents, providing services to Fortune 500 companies, governments, and enterprises across diverse industries.

Cost-Effective Solutions: Leveraging India's cost-competitive advantage, these companies have offered high-quality services at a fraction of the cost of their Western counterparts, making India the go-to destination for IT outsourcing.

Expertise Across Domains: These firms excel in areas such as software development, IT consulting, business process outsourcing (BPO), and process automation. From banking and finance to healthcare and retail, their domain-specific expertise allows them to cater to diverse client needs.

Global Delivery Model: Indian IT companies pioneered the global delivery model, combining onshore and offshore services to ensure seamless and efficient project execution. This model has become the industry standard, further cementing India's leadership in IT outsourcing.

Innovation and Value Addition: Beyond Cost Arbitrage

India's IT industry has evolved far beyond its initial value proposition of cost arbitrage. Today, it is a hub of innovation, leveraging cutting-edge technologies to deliver value-added solutions that drive transformative change for clients.

Adoption of Emerging Technologies: Indian IT firms are at the forefront of adopting and implementing technologies like **artificial intelligence (AI)**, **machine learning**, **cloud computing**, and **Internet of Things (IoT)**. These technologies enable businesses to automate processes, gain deeper insights through data analytics, and enhance operational efficiency.

Focus on Research and Development: Major IT firms have established innovation labs and R&D centers dedicated to exploring next-generation technologies. These centers focus on developing proprietary tools and platforms that give clients a competitive edge.

Custom Solutions for Global Clients: By moving beyond one-size-fits-all services, Indian IT companies now offer tailored solutions that address specific business challenges. This ability to innovate and adapt has elevated their role from service providers to strategic partners.

Digital Transformation Partners: Shaping the Future of Business

Indian IT companies have become pivotal in enabling digital transformation for global enterprises. As businesses face the imperative to modernize and stay competitive in a digital-first world, Indian firms are leading the charge with comprehensive solutions.

End-to-End Services: From developing digital platforms and implementing advanced analytics to deploying enterprise resource planning (ERP) systems and migrating to cloud infrastructure, Indian IT firms provide holistic support for digital transformation journeys.

Agility in Rapidly Evolving Markets: The fast-paced evolution of technology requires businesses to stay ahead of the curve. Indian IT firms are known for their agility, helping clients adapt quickly to changing market demands through real-time solutions.

Strengthening Global Enterprises: These firms are not just vendors but long-term partners for global enterprises. Their role extends to shaping strategies, improving customer experiences, and enhancing overall business performance, making them indispensable in the era of digital transformation.

The IT Industry's Role in India's Growth Story

The consistent growth and adaptability of India's IT industry underscore its strategic importance to the nation's economic and global standing. Its contributions go beyond economic metrics, driving technological advancements, creating millions of jobs, and uplifting India's reputation as a global technology leader.

The sector's success is also a testament to India's ability to deliver excellence on a global scale, combining technical expertise, innovation, and customer-centricity. As the industry continues to evolve, its role in shaping the future of global business will only grow stronger, reinforcing India's position as a technology powerhouse.

In the section ahead, we will explore how India's prowess in emerging technologies and its vibrant startup ecosystem further enhance its role as a technology magnet, offering unparalleled opportunities for investors and innovators alike.

Opportunities in Emerging Technologies

India's proactive adoption of emerging technologies is revolutionizing its economic landscape and positioning the nation as a global hub for technological innovation. These advancements are not only transforming traditional industries but also creating new frontiers for investors, entrepreneurs, and enterprises. Below is an in-depth exploration of key opportunities in emerging technologies and their transformative impact on India's economy.

Artificial Intelligence (AI): Transforming Industries

Artificial intelligence (AI) is driving a paradigm shift across sectors in India, enabling smarter decision-making, automation, and enhanced user experiences.

Revolutionizing Key Sectors:

✓ In **healthcare**, AI-powered tools are improving diagnostic accuracy, enabling remote patient monitoring, and streamlining hospital management systems. Startups like Niramai and Qure.ai are leveraging AI for early detection of diseases.

✓ In **education**, AI-driven platforms like BYJU'S are personalizing learning experiences for students, ensuring tailored content delivery based on individual needs.

✓ In **manufacturing**, AI is optimizing supply chains, reducing production downtime, and enabling predictive maintenance of machinery.

Government Initiatives: The Indian government's *National AI Strategy* emphasizes research, adoption, and capacity building in AI. This initiative aims to make India a global leader in AI applications, research, and development, attracting investment and fostering innovation.

Global Investments: Tech giants like Google, Microsoft, and IBM are investing heavily in India's AI ecosystem, recognizing the country's talent pool and innovation potential.

Internet of Things (IoT): Connecting the Future

The Internet of Things (IoT) is reshaping industries by enabling devices and systems to communicate, share data, and operate more efficiently.

Accelerating Adoption Across Sectors:

✓ In **agriculture**, IoT solutions like smart irrigation systems and soil sensors are improving crop yields and reducing water usage.

✓ In **smart cities**, IoT-powered applications are modernizing urban infrastructure, from intelligent traffic management systems to energy-efficient street lighting.

✓ In **industrial automation**, IoT-enabled devices are enhancing factory efficiency, reducing operational costs, and minimizing human errors.

The Smart Cities Mission: India's *Smart Cities Mission* integrates IoT technologies to improve urban living conditions. Projects in cities like Pune, Bengaluru, and Surat use IoT for waste management, water distribution, and public safety.

Startups and Collaborations: Indian startups like Zenatix and Thingstel are developing IoT solutions for industries, attracting collaborations with multinational corporations. The government's focus on digital infrastructure further accelerates IoT adoption, opening avenues for both domestic and foreign investments.

Blockchain: Redefining Trust and Transparency

Blockchain technology is being rapidly adopted in India, offering solutions that ensure transparency, security, and efficiency across various domains.

Applications Across Industries:

✓ In **financial services**, blockchain is enabling secure digital payments, reducing fraud, and streamlining cross-border transactions.

✓ In **supply chain management**, blockchain is ensuring traceability and transparency in logistics, helping businesses monitor product journeys in real time.

✓ In **digital identity verification**, blockchain-based systems like Aadhaar are providing secure and tamper-proof solutions for identity management.

Government and Private Sector Initiatives: Indian states like Telangana and Maharashtra are experimenting with blockchain for land record management and e-governance. Private enterprises like Tech Mahindra and Infosys are developing blockchain-based solutions for global clients.

Global Interest: The scalability and potential of blockchain in India are attracting interest from international tech companies and investors, positioning the country as a pioneer in blockchain applications.

Quantum Computing: The Next Frontier

Quantum computing, though still in its infancy, is gaining momentum in India. Its potential to solve complex problems at unprecedented speeds makes it a game-changer for industries like cryptography, pharmaceuticals, and materials science.

Research and Development: Leading institutions like the Indian Institute of Science (IISc) and the Indian Institutes of Technology (IITs) are conducting cutting-edge research in quantum computing. Government initiatives like the National Mission on Quantum Technologies and Applications (NM-QTA) aim to develop quantum infrastructure and train talent.

Applications Across Domains:

✓ In **cryptography**, quantum technologies offer breakthroughs in secure communication and encryption.

✓ In **pharmaceuticals**, quantum computing accelerates drug discovery by simulating complex molecular structures.

✓ In **logistics and optimization**, quantum algorithms enhance resource allocation and route planning.

Corporate Investments: Companies like IBM and Google are collaborating with Indian research institutions to develop quantum applications tailored for global markets.

India's Role as a Global Hub for Innovation

The rapid adoption of these emerging technologies reflects India's ambition to become a global leader in innovation. The combination of government support, a vast talent pool, and an entrepreneurial spirit ensures that India remains at the forefront of technological advancements.

These technologies not only hold the potential to transform industries but also pave the way for new investment opportunities. For investors, India's thriving ecosystem offers a fertile ground to capitalize on the convergence of innovation, scalability, and impact.

In summary, India's embrace of emerging technologies represents a defining chapter in its economic evolution. From AI and IoT to blockchain and quantum computing, these advancements are reshaping industries and creating unparalleled opportunities for businesses and investors. As these technologies mature, they promise to position India not only as a leader in technological innovation but also as a global destination for transformative solutions that address the world's most pressing challenges.

Startup India: Unicorns, Accelerators, and the Venture Capital Ecosystem

India's startup ecosystem has become a global phenomenon, ranking third worldwide in terms of the number of unicorns—privately held startups valued at over $1 billion. With more than 100 unicorns as of 2024 and a rapidly growing number of innovative ventures, the country has established itself as a hotbed of entrepreneurship and creativity. From fintech and edtech to agritech and healthtech, startups in India are solving real-world problems while driving economic growth, job creation, and technological innovation.

The Startup India Initiative: A Catalyst for Entrepreneurship

Launched in 2016, the *Startup India* initiative has played a pivotal role in fostering a thriving culture of entrepreneurship in India. This government-led program provides a comprehensive support system designed to nurture startups at every stage of their journey.

Funding and Tax Benefits: Under this initiative, startups enjoy tax exemptions for three consecutive years, access to government-backed funding schemes, and reduced compliance requirements, enabling them to focus on innovation and growth. The *Fund of Funds for Startups (FFS)*, managed by SIDBI, has allocated billions to support early-stage ventures.

Ease of Doing Business: Simplified processes for registering startups, obtaining intellectual property rights, and accessing funding have significantly reduced barriers to entry. Online platforms like the Startup India portal offer a one-stop solution for entrepreneurs to avail of these benefits.

Sectoral Inclusivity: The program encourages startups across diverse sectors, from technology and agriculture to social impact and sustainability, ensuring that innovation reaches all corners of the economy.

The *Startup India* initiative has not only empowered entrepreneurs but also enhanced India's reputation as a global leader in fostering startup ecosystems.

Unicorn Boom: Scaling New Heights

The rise of Indian unicorns is a testament to the country's ability to create businesses that are scalable, impactful, and globally competitive.

Iconic Unicorns: Companies like **BYJU'S**, **Paytm**, **Zomato**, **Flipkart**, and **Nykaa** have become household names, disrupting traditional business models and transforming industries.

- ✓ **BYJU'S**: Revolutionizing education with personalized and tech-driven learning solutions.

✓ **Paytm**: Driving financial inclusion through digital payments and innovative financial services.

✓ **Zomato**: Redefining food delivery and restaurant discovery.

Sectoral Diversity: Unicorns in India span a wide range of sectors, including fintech, e-commerce, healthtech, edtech, and logistics, reflecting the ecosystem's ability to cater to varied market needs.

Global Influence: These unicorns not only dominate the domestic market but also expand internationally, showcasing India's capacity to produce global players. They serve as role models for aspiring entrepreneurs, inspiring a new generation to innovate and scale their ventures.

Accelerators and Incubators: Nurturing Early-Stage Startups

India's robust network of accelerators and incubators plays a crucial role in nurturing startups during their formative stages. These organizations provide entrepreneurs with mentorship, resources, and access to networks, ensuring their ideas have the support needed to grow into successful businesses.

Leading Accelerators: Programs like Y Combinator, Techstars, and Indian accelerators such as **Nasscom's 10,000 Startups** and **Indian Angel Network (IAN)** are instrumental in guiding startups.

Incubators Across India: State-level initiatives, university-led incubators, and private organizations offer startups office spaces, technical expertise, and business development support. For example, IITs and IIMs have established incubators that focus on technology and innovation-driven ventures.

Co-working Spaces: Spaces like WeWork, 91Springboard, and Innov8 provide startups with cost-effective infrastructure, fostering a collaborative environment that encourages knowledge sharing and partnerships.

By bridging the gap between ideas and execution, these accelerators and incubators ensure that startups have a strong foundation for success.

Venture Capital and Private Equity: Fuelling Innovation

India's thriving venture capital (VC) and private equity (PE) ecosystem provides the financial lifeline that startups need to scale and succeed.

Domestic and International Investments: VC funds, both domestic and global, are pouring into Indian startups at unprecedented rates. Firms like Sequoia Capital, Tiger Global, Accel Partners, and SoftBank are actively investing in high-growth ventures.

Sector-Specific Funding:

✓ **Fintech**: Startups like Razorpay and PhonePe have attracted significant funding due to the growing demand for digital payment solutions.

✓ **Edtech**: Companies like BYJU'S and Unacademy have benefited from increased investments during the shift to online learning.

✓ **Healthtech**: Startups like Practo and PharmEasy have gained traction with their tech-enabled healthcare services.

Government-Backed Funds: Initiatives like the *Fund of Funds for Startups* and sectoral funds for biotech, agriculture, and defense have catalyzed the availability of capital, especially for early-stage ventures.

This influx of capital has not only enabled startups to expand but has also created an environment conducive to risk-taking and innovation.

Solving Real-World Problems with Scalable Solutions

India's startup ecosystem is not just about wealth creation; it is about solving pressing challenges with scalable and impactful solutions.

Social Impact Startups: Startups like SELCO (solar lighting) and Frontier Markets (last-mile distribution) are addressing issues related to energy access, rural livelihoods, and financial inclusion.

Sustainability and Climate Solutions: Ventures in clean energy, waste management, and sustainable agriculture are contributing to India's environmental goals while generating economic value.

Technology for Good: Startups are leveraging AI, IoT, and blockchain to provide solutions in healthcare, education, and governance, ensuring inclusive growth and societal impact.

In conclusion, India's startup ecosystem represents a dynamic blend of innovation, entrepreneurship, and opportunity. From the government's proactive support under the *Startup India* initiative to the rise of unicorns that set global benchmarks, the ecosystem has created a thriving environment for new ideas to flourish. The robust infrastructure of accelerators, incubators, and venture capital ensures that startups can transform their visions into reality.

This ecosystem's focus on addressing real-world problems with scalable solutions makes India a magnet for global investors. As the country continues to nurture its entrepreneurial spirit, it is poised to lead the next wave of global innovation, reinforcing its position as a technology and startup powerhouse.

Conclusion

India's technology sector is a powerhouse of innovation, growth, and global influence. It seamlessly combines the strengths of a well-established IT services industry, a burgeoning focus on cutting-edge technologies, and a thriving startup ecosystem. This synergy has transformed India into a magnet for technology-driven investments, drawing attention from global players seeking to tap into its talent, creativity, and entrepreneurial spirit.

The dominance of India's IT industry as a trusted outsourcing hub has evolved into a broader narrative of technological leadership. Beyond cost efficiency, Indian firms are driving transformative changes by leveraging artificial intelligence, blockchain, IoT, and quantum computing. These advancements are not only redefining traditional industries but also creating entirely new avenues for growth and innovation. Initiatives like *Digital India* and the *National AI Strategy* highlight the government's forward-thinking approach, ensuring that India remains at the forefront of technological progress.

India's startup ecosystem adds another dimension to its technological magnetism. With more than 100 unicorns and countless innovative ventures, Indian startups are addressing global challenges and creating scalable solutions across fintech, edtech, healthtech, and beyond. Supported by accelerators, incubators, and a vibrant venture capital network, these startups are reshaping industries and enhancing India's reputation as a global innovation hub.

The country's adaptability and alignment with global trends further reinforce its appeal. India is not just participating in the global digital revolution—it is helping lead it. From shaping digital transformation strategies for global enterprises to spearheading advancements in emerging technologies, India's technological prowess continues to make waves on the world stage.

As we explore India's sectoral strengths in subsequent chapters, the themes of innovation, resilience, and opportunity highlighted in this chapter will remain central. India's technology sector is more than a driver of economic growth—it is a beacon of what's possible when talent, vision, and policy converge. For investors, entrepreneurs, and enterprises, India's technological landscape offers an unmatched opportunity to be part of a future defined by innovation and global impact.

4. The Manufacturing Magnet: Industry 4.0 and Beyond

"India: Where Innovation Fuels Industry"

India's manufacturing sector is at the forefront of a transformative journey, shaped by visionary government initiatives, rapid technological advancements, and a renewed emphasis on self-reliance. From the groundbreaking *Make in India* campaign to the ambitious *Atmanirbhar Bharat* initiative, the country has strategically positioned itself as a global manufacturing magnet that seamlessly blends cost efficiency with cutting-edge innovation.

With abundant opportunities across high-growth industries such as automotive, electric vehicles (EVs), aerospace, and consumer durables, India is steadily carving its place as a global manufacturing powerhouse. This evolution is not just about producing goods—it's about redefining manufacturing to align with the principles of Industry 4.0, creating a future-ready industrial landscape that attracts investment, fosters innovation, and drives sustainable growth.

The Rise of India as a Manufacturing Hub: From "Make in India" to "Atmanirbhar Bharat"

India's manufacturing sector has experienced a remarkable transformation over the past decade, thanks to visionary initiatives aimed at bolstering domestic production, attracting foreign investment, and generating employment. This journey began with the launch of the *Make in India* campaign in 2014, which set the stage for India's emergence as a global manufacturing hub. Building on this foundation, the *Atmanirbhar Bharat* (Self-Reliant India) initiative, introduced during the pandemic, further strengthened the focus on self-reliance and reduced import dependency, aligning India's goals with global manufacturing trends.

Make in India: Laying the Foundation for Industrial Growth

The *Make in India* initiative marked a turning point for the country's industrial ambitions. Designed to position India as a global manufacturing leader, the program targeted 25 key sectors and implemented reforms to make doing business easier and more efficient.

Sectoral Focus: The initiative concentrated on high-potential sectors, including **automobiles**, **textiles**, **electronics**, **defense**, and **renewable energy**, with the aim of making India a production powerhouse.

Reforms and Reductions: To attract investment, the government streamlined bureaucratic processes, reduced regulatory hurdles, and introduced policies that encouraged ease of business. Tax incentives, simplified licensing, and digitized approval processes became cornerstones of the campaign.

Boost in FDI: The results of these efforts were evident in the record-breaking foreign direct investment (FDI) inflows. In 2023-24, India attracted over $81 billion in FDI, much of it directed towards manufacturing sectors. This inflow has led to the establishment of production facilities by global giants like Foxconn, Samsung, and Boeing.

Global Manufacturing Partnerships: Collaboration with multinational corporations enabled the transfer of advanced technologies and practices, raising the standards of Indian manufacturing. The program also emphasized skill development through initiatives like Skill India to ensure a capable workforce for these industries.

Atmanirbhar Bharat: Strengthening Self-Reliance

The pandemic-induced disruptions in global supply chains highlighted the importance of self-reliance, giving rise to the *Atmanirbhar Bharat* initiative. This program built on the foundation laid by *Make in India*, but with an added emphasis on reducing dependency on imports and fostering local innovation and production.

Indigenous Production: The initiative promotes manufacturing in critical sectors like **defense**, **pharmaceuticals**, and **electronics**, encouraging domestic companies to meet national and global demand. For instance, India now produces significant portions of its defense equipment domestically, reducing its reliance on imports.

Public-Private Partnerships: The initiative actively involves private players through public-private partnerships (PPPs), enabling them to contribute to infrastructure, technology, and expertise. Companies like Tata and Mahindra are now integral to India's defense and automotive sectors.

Aligning with Global Trends: India's focus on self-reliance aligns with global trends like **reshoring** and **nearshoring**, as companies seek to diversify supply chains. This shift positions India as a preferred destination for global manufacturing operations.

PLI Schemes: Under the umbrella of *Atmanirbhar Bharat*, the **Production Linked Incentive (PLI)** schemes have been introduced to incentivize manufacturers in sectors like electronics, renewable energy, and automobiles. These schemes offer financial benefits based on production levels, attracting both domestic and international players.

A Preferred Destination for Global Manufacturing

Together, *Make in India* and *Atmanirbhar Bharat* are transforming India into a global manufacturing hub by leveraging its unique advantages:

Skilled Workforce: With a young and talented labor pool, India provides cost-effective yet high-quality production capabilities, making it a competitive choice for global manufacturers.

Competitive Costs: India offers one of the lowest manufacturing costs among major economies, further enhanced by government incentives and supportive policies.

Policy Support and Infrastructure Development: Industrial corridors like the Delhi-Mumbai Industrial Corridor (DMIC) and dedicated Special Economic Zones (SEZs) provide world-class infrastructure and connectivity, reducing operational challenges for businesses.

In conclusion, the synergy between *Make in India* and *Atmanirbhar Bharat* has not only revitalized India's manufacturing sector but has also positioned the country as a reliable and attractive destination for global manufacturing investments. By fostering innovation, streamlining processes, and focusing on self-reliance, India is creating a manufacturing ecosystem that is future-ready and globally competitive. As the momentum continues, India's journey toward becoming a global manufacturing powerhouse stands as a testament to the power of strategic planning and visionary leadership.

Opportunities in Automotive, EVs, Aerospace, and Consumer Durables

India's manufacturing sector is a dynamic powerhouse with diverse opportunities across high-potential industries. Automotive, electric vehicles (EVs), aerospace, and consumer durables are at the forefront of this growth, supported by robust government initiatives, a skilled workforce, and increasing domestic and global demand. These sectors showcase India's ability to cater to emerging global trends while fostering self-reliance and innovation.

Automotive and Electric Vehicles (EVs)

India has firmly established itself as a significant player in the global automotive market and is rapidly advancing in the EV space, driven by policy support, innovation, and investment.

Automotive Hub: India is the **world's fourth-largest automotive market**, producing vehicles and components for both domestic and international markets.

Major players like **Tata Motors**, **Mahindra**, and **Maruti Suzuki** are leading the charge with innovations in passenger vehicles, commercial vehicles, and off-road vehicles.

India is a leading exporter of vehicles and components, catering to regions like Europe, Africa, and Asia. Exports of auto components alone reached $20 billion in 2023, underscoring the sector's global impact.

The country's focus on sustainability and efficiency has driven advancements in hybrid and alternative fuel vehicles, further boosting its competitive edge.

EV Revolution: India is at the forefront of the global shift toward electric mobility. The **Faster Adoption and Manufacturing of Hybrid and Electric Vehicles (FAME)** scheme offers subsidies and tax benefits to promote EV adoption and production. Domestic companies like **Ola Electric** and **Ather Energy** are pioneering innovations in electric scooters and bikes, while startups are developing EV charging infrastructure.

Global giants, including **Tesla**, are exploring opportunities to establish production facilities in India, drawn by the country's market potential and cost advantages. By 2030, India aims to electrify 30% of its vehicle fleet, creating significant opportunities for battery production, EV manufacturing, and ancillary services.

Aerospace and Defense

India's aerospace and defense industries are undergoing a rapid transformation, supported by strategic policies, global partnerships, and indigenous innovation.

Expanding Aerospace Capabilities: India is emerging as a global aerospace hub, with increasing investments in manufacturing and R&D. Government policies such as raising the **FDI cap in defense to 74%** have encouraged collaborations with global players like **Boeing**, **Airbus**, and **Lockheed Martin**. The country's focus on indigenous production is evident in projects like **HAL's Tejas fighter jet**, **DRDO's missile systems**, and the **Advanced Medium Combat Aircraft (AMCA)** program. Aerospace manufacturing clusters in Bengaluru, Hyderabad, and Pune are driving growth by integrating advanced technologies like 3D printing and robotics.

Defense Production: India's defense manufacturing is gaining momentum under the *Make in India* and *Atmanirbhar Bharat* initiatives. India is now producing significant defense equipment domestically, including artillery systems, drones, and naval vessels. Partnerships with domestic companies like **Bharat Electronics Limited (BEL)** and **Tata Advanced Systems** are enhancing production capabilities and reducing dependency on imports.

Consumer Durables

India's consumer durables sector is witnessing robust growth, driven by rising incomes, urbanization, and a growing middle class.

Demand Surge: The expanding middle class, expected to constitute 70% of India's population by 2030, has fueled demand for electronics, household appliances, and smart devices. Products like air conditioners, washing machines, and refrigerators are becoming essential in urban and semi-urban households, creating vast opportunities for manufacturers.

Domestic Manufacturing: India has become a hub for electronics manufacturing, particularly in smartphones and consumer electronics. Global giants like **Foxconn**, **Samsung**, and **Apple** have established large-scale production facilities in India, driven by initiatives like the **Production Linked Incentive (PLI)** scheme. Domestic brands such as **Micromax** and **Lava** are also contributing to the sector's growth, leveraging cost-effective production and local supply chains.

Technological Integration: The integration of IoT and smart technologies in consumer durables has further enhanced demand, as consumers seek innovative and energy-efficient solutions. Companies are investing in R&D to develop products tailored to the preferences of Indian consumers, creating a competitive and diverse market.

India's Competitive Edge in Manufacturing

Across these industries, India's competitive advantages include:

✓ **Skilled Workforce**: India boasts a large pool of engineers and technicians, providing the expertise needed for advanced manufacturing.

✓ **Cost Efficiency**: The cost of manufacturing in India is significantly lower than in many other countries, attracting global players.

✓ **Policy Support**: Programs like *Make in India*, *Atmanirbhar Bharat*, and the PLI schemes provide financial incentives, reduce compliance burdens, and promote exports.

In short, India's manufacturing base offers immense opportunities in automotive, EVs, aerospace, and consumer durables, underpinned by robust policy frameworks and a growing domestic market. With a clear vision for the future, strong global partnerships, and a commitment to innovation, these industries are driving India's emergence as a global manufacturing leader. For investors and businesses, India represents a dynamic ecosystem poised for exponential growth and long-term success.

Role of Special Economic Zones (SEZs) and Industrial Corridors

India's manufacturing sector is bolstered by a well-designed network of Special Economic Zones (SEZs) and industrial corridors that enhance competitiveness and attract investment. These initiatives create world-class infrastructure, simplify regulatory processes, and offer targeted incentives to businesses, enabling them to thrive in a globally competitive environment. Together, SEZs and industrial corridors play a critical role in transforming India into a manufacturing magnet.

Special Economic Zones (SEZs): Catalysts for Growth

Special Economic Zones (SEZs) in India serve as hubs of industrial activity, offering a conducive environment for manufacturing and exports. Designed to encourage foreign investment and promote economic growth, SEZs provide companies with numerous benefits and advantages.

Favorable Business Environment: SEZs offer tax incentives, including exemptions from customs duties and income tax, and streamlined procedures for setting up and operating businesses. These zones are equipped with state-of-the-art infrastructure, making them attractive for both domestic and international investors.

Prominent SEZs:

- ✓ **Santacruz Electronics Export Processing Zone (SEEPZ)**, Mumbai: A pioneer in India's SEZ landscape, SEEPZ specializes in electronics and gem manufacturing. It has played a crucial role in boosting high-tech manufacturing and exports.

- ✓ **Nokia SEZ**, Tamil Nadu: Focused on electronics and telecommunications manufacturing, this SEZ has been instrumental in attracting global companies like Foxconn and creating a robust supply chain ecosystem.

Sectoral Focus and Innovation: SEZs cater to various industries, from IT and electronics to textiles and pharmaceuticals. This sector-specific focus ensures that companies can access skilled labor, advanced technology, and industry-specific resources within the zones.

SEZs not only promote exports and industrial activity but also generate employment and drive regional development, contributing significantly to India's economic growth.

Industrial Corridors: Connecting Growth Centers

India's industrial corridors are massive infrastructure projects aimed at connecting economic hubs, reducing logistics costs, and boosting manufacturing efficiency. These corridors integrate transport networks, industrial clusters, and smart cities, creating a seamless environment for businesses to operate and expand.

Delhi-Mumbai Industrial Corridor (DMIC): One of the largest infrastructure projects globally, the DMIC spans over 1,500 kilometers, linking Delhi and Mumbai. It focuses on creating high-tech industrial zones equipped with smart cities, state-of-the-art logistics hubs, and efficient transport networks. The corridor has attracted significant foreign investment and is expected to contribute 15% of India's GDP once fully operational.

Chennai-Bengaluru Industrial Corridor (CBIC): This corridor aims to enhance industrial activity and connectivity in southern India, spanning the technology and automotive hubs of Chennai and Bengaluru. It supports sectors such as electronics, IT, and automotive manufacturing, making the region a powerhouse for advanced manufacturing and technology-driven industries.

Amritsar-Kolkata Industrial Corridor (AKIC): Designed to boost industrial growth in northern and eastern India, the AKIC connects major economic centers, fostering trade and investment in the region. The corridor supports industries like steel, textiles, and food processing, creating opportunities for development in historically underrepresented areas.

Impact on Manufacturing Competitiveness

SEZs and industrial corridors are instrumental in making India a competitive destination for manufacturing by addressing key challenges and enhancing efficiency:

Investment Attraction: These initiatives offer a one-stop solution for businesses, providing the infrastructure, incentives, and regulatory support needed to attract significant foreign and domestic investment.

Efficient Logistics: Integrated transport networks and logistics hubs reduce transit times and costs, ensuring that goods reach domestic and international markets quickly and efficiently.

Regional Development: By creating economic hubs across the country, SEZs and industrial corridors drive balanced regional development, reducing economic disparities and boosting employment.

Technology and Innovation: High-tech zones within SEZs and industrial corridors foster innovation, encouraging companies to adopt advanced manufacturing techniques and technologies.

In conclusion, India's network of SEZs and industrial corridors is a cornerstone of its manufacturing strategy, offering businesses a robust framework to grow and thrive. These initiatives combine world-class infrastructure, targeted incentives, and seamless connectivity to create an environment that attracts investment and enhances competitiveness. As India continues to expand and develop its industrial infrastructure, SEZs and industrial corridors will play a pivotal role in shaping the country's journey as a global manufacturing leader. For investors and businesses, these zones and corridors represent unparalleled opportunities to tap into India's industrial potential and contribute to its economic growth.

Industry 4.0: The Future of Manufacturing in India

India's manufacturing sector is at the forefront of a technological revolution, ushering in the era of Industry 4.0. This new wave of manufacturing innovation is characterized by the integration of advanced technologies such as robotics, the Internet of Things (IoT), artificial intelligence (AI), and data analytics into industrial processes. These advancements are not only improving efficiency and productivity but also redefining the way goods are produced, paving the way for India to lead the global manufacturing landscape in the 21st century.

Smart Factories: Redefining Efficiency and Quality

Smart factories lie at the heart of Industry 4.0, leveraging automation, real-time monitoring, and advanced analytics to create highly efficient manufacturing environments.

Automation and Robotics: Indian manufacturers are adopting robotics to streamline assembly lines, handle repetitive tasks, and improve precision. Collaborative robots (cobots) are being deployed to work alongside humans, enhancing productivity while reducing labor-intensive processes.

Real-Time Monitoring: Advanced IoT systems enable real-time tracking of operations, providing manufacturers with actionable insights into production processes. By identifying bottlenecks and inefficiencies, factories can optimize operations and reduce waste.

Improved Product Quality: With the help of AI-driven quality control systems, manufacturers can detect defects early in the production process, ensuring consistent quality standards and reducing rework costs.

Smart factories are setting new benchmarks for operational efficiency and product excellence, enabling Indian manufacturers to compete on a global scale.

Predictive Maintenance: Reducing Downtime and Costs

Predictive maintenance is revolutionizing how factories manage equipment and machinery, ensuring minimal disruptions and maximum efficiency.

IoT Sensors for Monitoring: IoT-enabled sensors continuously collect data on machine performance, detecting anomalies and potential issues before they lead to failures.

AI-Driven Insights: AI algorithms analyze data to predict maintenance needs, allowing manufacturers to schedule repairs proactively. This approach minimizes unplanned downtime, extends the lifespan of equipment, and reduces maintenance costs.

Cost Savings: By transitioning from reactive to predictive maintenance, Indian manufacturers are achieving significant cost savings while ensuring uninterrupted production. This capability is particularly critical in industries such as automotive, aerospace, and electronics, where downtime can lead to substantial financial losses.

Sustainability: Green Manufacturing for a Greener Future

Sustainability is becoming a core focus of Industry 4.0 in India, as manufacturers adopt environmentally friendly practices to align with global sustainability goals.

Renewable Energy Integration: Indian factories are increasingly utilizing renewable energy sources such as solar and wind to power their operations, reducing dependence on fossil fuels. This shift is supported by government incentives and programs promoting renewable energy adoption.

Energy Efficiency: Advanced energy management systems, driven by IoT and AI, help manufacturers optimize energy consumption, lowering operational costs and reducing their carbon footprint.

Circular Economy Practices: Companies are adopting circular manufacturing models that emphasize recycling, reusing materials, and minimizing waste. For example, the automotive and electronics industries are focusing on sustainable materials and recycling components.

Eco-Friendly Products: Indian manufacturers are increasingly designing eco-friendly products that cater to environmentally conscious consumers, strengthening their competitive edge in global markets.

Sustainable manufacturing not only aligns with environmental goals but also enhances India's reputation as a responsible global manufacturing leader.

India's Position in Global Industry 4.0

India is uniquely positioned to capitalize on Industry 4.0 due to its growing technological capabilities, large talent pool, and supportive policy environment.

Government Initiatives: Programs such as *Make in India* and *Digital India* are driving digital transformation in the manufacturing sector, enabling companies to adopt Industry 4.0 technologies seamlessly.

Skill Development: Initiatives like *Skill India* and partnerships with global tech companies are ensuring that India's workforce is equipped with the skills required to operate and manage advanced manufacturing technologies.

Startups and Innovation: India's vibrant startup ecosystem is playing a crucial role in developing Industry 4.0 solutions, from AI-powered analytics tools to IoT platforms designed for manufacturing.

Cost-Competitiveness: India's cost advantage, coupled with its ability to implement cutting-edge technologies, makes it an attractive destination for global manufacturers looking to establish Industry 4.0 facilities.

In conclusion, Industry 4.0 is revolutionizing India's manufacturing sector, enabling it to achieve unprecedented levels of efficiency, sustainability, and innovation. By embracing technologies such as robotics, IoT, AI, and data analytics, Indian manufacturers are transforming their operations into smart, connected ecosystems that are ready to compete globally.

With its strategic advantages, robust policy support, and commitment to sustainable practices, India is well-positioned to lead the next phase of global manufacturing innovation. As the adoption of Industry 4.0 accelerates, India's manufacturing sector is set to become a key driver of economic growth and a model for the future of global industry.

Conclusion

India's manufacturing sector stands on the brink of a transformative era, marked by strategic foresight, technological evolution, and a steadfast commitment to self-reliance. The nation's ability to harness these elements has not only revitalized its traditional industrial base but also positioned it as a beacon for global manufacturing investments.

From the thriving automotive industry and the burgeoning EV market to the rapidly advancing aerospace and consumer durables sectors, India offers a landscape rich with opportunities. The integration of modern manufacturing practices through initiatives like Industry 4.0 has introduced a new dimension of efficiency, innovation, and sustainability. These advancements, coupled with targeted policies such as *Make in India* and *Atmanirbhar Bharat*, reflect India's ambition to become a leader in the global manufacturing ecosystem.

Infrastructure plays a pivotal role in this transformation. Special Economic Zones (SEZs) and industrial corridors such as the Delhi-Mumbai Industrial Corridor (DMIC) and Chennai-Bengaluru Industrial Corridor are creating an interconnected, streamlined environment for manufacturing and logistics. These zones not only attract significant investments but also reduce operational complexities, ensuring India's competitiveness on the global stage.

What truly sets India apart is its ability to align its manufacturing ambitions with global trends in sustainability and innovation. The adoption of green manufacturing practices, the integration of renewable energy, and the focus on creating environmentally friendly products demonstrate a future-ready approach that appeals to global investors and partners.

As India continues to refine its manufacturing landscape, the magnetism highlighted in this chapter serves as a testament to the country's potential to lead the next phase of industrial innovation. For investors, this is a critical juncture to engage with India's dynamic manufacturing ecosystem, participate in its growth story, and capitalize on the vast opportunities that lie ahead. India is not just preparing for the future of manufacturing—it is actively shaping it.

5. The Green Magnet: Renewable Energy and Sustainability

"India: Pioneering the Path to a Sustainable Future"

India has emerged as a trailblazer in renewable energy and sustainability, reshaping its energy landscape to harmonize environmental objectives with economic growth. With an unwavering commitment to solar, wind, and green hydrogen, the country is setting new global standards in clean energy generation and adoption. These efforts have unlocked vast investment opportunities in clean technology, sustainable infrastructure, and environmentally responsible business ventures, underpinned by India's dedication to Environmental, Social, and Governance (ESG) principles.

This chapter delves into India's renewable energy achievements, explores the burgeoning prospects in sustainability-focused investments, and highlights the critical role of ESG compliance in driving the nation toward a sustainable and inclusive future.

India's Leadership in Renewable Energy: Solar, Wind, and Green Hydrogen

India's renewable energy sector is among the most dynamic and rapidly growing in the world, driven by ambitious goals, innovative projects, and robust government support. The country has set a target of achieving 500 GW of renewable energy capacity by 2030, making it a global leader in clean energy transformation. Significant progress has already been made in solar and wind energy, while green hydrogen is emerging as a promising frontier for future growth. These efforts underscore India's commitment to addressing global climate challenges while meeting its energy security needs.

Solar Power: Harnessing the Sun's Potential

India has emerged as a powerhouse in solar energy, ranking among the top countries globally in installed solar capacity. With over 70 GW of capacity as of 2024, solar power forms the backbone of India's renewable energy strategy.

Large-Scale Solar Parks: India's success in developing mega solar projects is exemplified by landmarks like the **Bhadla Solar Park** in Rajasthan, the world's largest solar park with a capacity of 2,245 MW. Similarly, the **Pavagada Solar Park** in Karnataka, spread across 13,000 acres, reflects India's ability to scale up solar infrastructure efficiently.

Decentralized Solar Systems: Rooftop solar installations and off-grid solar solutions are gaining traction in urban and rural areas, supported by government initiatives like the **Kusum Scheme**, which promotes solar-powered irrigation and rural electrification. Subsidies and incentives for residential solar installations are also encouraging widespread adoption.

International Collaboration: As a founding member of the **International Solar Alliance (ISA)**, India is leading global efforts to promote solar energy adoption. Collaborative projects with nations across Africa, Asia, and Europe are amplifying India's influence as a solar energy leader.

Wind Energy: Capturing Clean Kinetic Power

India's wind energy sector complements its solar initiatives, making it the fourth-largest producer of wind energy globally. The country has leveraged its geographic advantages to develop a robust wind energy ecosystem, with significant capacity in Tamil Nadu, Gujarat, and Maharashtra.

Onshore Wind Energy: Onshore wind farms in regions like **Kanyakumari** (Tamil Nadu) and **Bhuj** (Gujarat) are driving the production of clean, renewable power. Advanced technologies in turbine design and efficiency are further enhancing the potential of these projects.

Offshore Wind Energy: India's coastline offers immense opportunities for offshore wind energy development, with initial projects being explored in states like Gujarat and Tamil Nadu. Offshore wind farms have the potential to tap into higher and more consistent wind speeds, making them a valuable addition to India's renewable energy mix.

Hybrid Renewable Energy Projects: Combining wind and solar energy into hybrid projects is a growing trend in India, aimed at optimizing efficiency and ensuring grid stability. Hybrid systems reduce intermittency issues and enable better utilization of renewable resources.

Green Hydrogen: The Fuel of the Future

India is at the forefront of the green hydrogen revolution, recognizing its potential as a clean and versatile energy source. Green hydrogen, produced using renewable electricity, is emerging as a critical component of India's energy transition strategy.

National Hydrogen Mission: Launched to establish India as a global hub for green hydrogen production, the **National Hydrogen Mission** sets ambitious goals of producing 5 million metric tons of green hydrogen annually by 2030. This initiative aims to reduce India's dependence on fossil fuels and cut greenhouse gas emissions.

Industrial and Export Potential: Green hydrogen is poised to revolutionize industries such as steel, chemicals, and transportation, where decarbonization has been challenging. India's strategic geographic location and renewable energy capacity position it as a leading exporter of green hydrogen to markets in Europe and Asia.

Private Sector Investment: Leading corporations like **Reliance Industries**, **Adani Group**, and **Tata Power** are making substantial investments in green hydrogen production and related infrastructure. These efforts reflect strong private-sector engagement and confidence in the future of green hydrogen.

International Collaboration: India is partnering with global players to develop green hydrogen technologies and infrastructure, fostering innovation and accelerating adoption.

Driving the Energy Transition

India's integrated approach to solar, wind, and green hydrogen underscores its leadership in renewable energy. The country's renewable energy strategy is not only helping it meet domestic energy demands sustainably but also positioning it as a critical player in the global energy transition.

Economic Benefits: Renewable energy projects are creating jobs, reducing energy costs, and fostering economic development, particularly in rural areas.

Environmental Impact: By replacing fossil fuels with renewable sources, India is making significant strides in reducing carbon emissions and combating climate change.

Energy Security: Expanding renewable energy capacity enhances India's energy independence and reduces reliance on imported fuels, contributing to long-term energy security.

Thus, India's leadership in renewable energy is a testament to its commitment to sustainability and innovation. With transformative projects in solar, wind, and green hydrogen, the country is paving the way for a cleaner and more resilient energy future. For investors and stakeholders, India's renewable energy sector offers unparalleled opportunities to contribute to and benefit from one of the most exciting energy transitions in the world.

Investment Opportunities in Clean Tech and Sustainable Infrastructure

India's transition to renewable energy and sustainable infrastructure is creating a wealth of investment opportunities across sectors. The focus on clean technology and infrastructure development is not only transforming India's energy landscape but also making it an attractive destination for global investors. From energy storage and electric mobility to smart cities and green buildings, the possibilities for innovation and growth are vast.

Clean Technology: Powering the Future

Clean technology, or cleantech, is at the forefront of India's renewable energy revolution, offering opportunities for innovation, efficiency, and scalability.

Energy Storage Solutions: As renewable energy generation scales up, efficient energy storage systems are becoming essential for balancing supply and demand. Indian companies and startups are developing advanced battery technologies, including lithium-ion and sodium-ion batteries, to support grid stability and electric mobility. Energy storage solutions like grid-scale battery systems and pumped hydro storage are attracting significant investment, with their potential to revolutionize energy management.

Electric Mobility: The shift to electric vehicles (EVs) is driving innovation in battery technology, charging infrastructure, and vehicle manufacturing. Startups like Ola Electric and Ather Energy are spearheading India's EV movement, while global players like Tesla are exploring production facilities in India. Government incentives under the *Faster Adoption and Manufacturing of*

Hybrid and Electric Vehicles (FAME) scheme provide additional support for the EV ecosystem.

Smart Grids and Digital Energy Management: Innovations in grid management technologies are enabling real-time monitoring and efficient distribution of renewable energy. Smart grids integrate renewable energy sources seamlessly into the grid, reducing transmission losses and improving reliability. Companies are investing in IoT-based solutions for energy monitoring and demand forecasting, creating a robust ecosystem for smart energy management. India's cleantech ecosystem is vibrant and growing, offering investors the chance to be part of transformative projects that have both economic and environmental benefits.

Sustainable Infrastructure: Building the Green Future

Sustainable infrastructure development is a cornerstone of India's renewable energy ambitions, creating investment opportunities across urban and rural landscapes.

Renewable Energy Projects: Large-scale solar parks, wind farms, and hydropower plants are driving India's renewable energy expansion. Projects like the **Bhadla Solar Park** and **Kurnool Ultra Mega Solar Park** have set global benchmarks, attracting investments from international development banks and private equity firms. Offshore wind farms along India's coastline are a burgeoning area for investment, with pilot projects in Gujarat and Tamil Nadu paving the way for large-scale development.

Green Buildings and Urban Sustainability: The demand for green buildings is rising, driven by urbanization and environmental awareness. Developers are incorporating energy-efficient designs, solar panels, rainwater harvesting systems, and waste management solutions into commercial and residential projects. Certification programs like **LEED (Leadership in Energy and Environmental Design)** are incentivizing sustainable construction practices.

Smart Cities Initiatives: India's Smart Cities Mission is integrating renewable energy and sustainability into urban planning. Investment opportunities abound in areas like urban transport (e-mobility and metro systems), waste management (recycling and waste-to-energy projects), and water systems (water recycling and desalination plants). Cities like Pune, Bengaluru, and Ahmedabad are becoming models of sustainable urbanization, attracting both domestic and foreign investors.

Sustainable infrastructure projects not only address environmental challenges but also create long-term value for investors, offering stable returns and contributing to India's economic growth.

Global Partnerships: Fostering Innovation and Collaboration

India's renewable energy journey is marked by strategic global collaborations that bring in technological expertise, financing, and market access.

Bilateral and Multilateral Partnerships: Collaborations with countries like the US, Germany, and Japan are advancing India's clean energy goals. These partnerships focus on technology transfer, joint research, and capacity building. Programs like the **Indo-German Energy Partnership** and the **US-India Strategic Clean Energy Partnership** have facilitated significant investments in solar, wind, and hydrogen projects.

Investment from Development Banks and Sovereign Wealth Funds: Institutions like the **World Bank**, **Asian Development Bank (ADB)**, and **Green Climate Fund** are financing renewable energy and sustainable infrastructure projects in India. Sovereign wealth funds from the Middle East and Europe are investing in India's clean energy sector, recognizing its potential for high returns and environmental impact.

Private Sector Engagement: Multinational corporations like Google, Microsoft, and Amazon are investing in India's renewable energy sector to meet their sustainability goals. These companies are entering power purchase agreements (PPAs) with Indian renewable energy providers, driving demand for clean energy.

Thus, India's transition to renewable energy and sustainable infrastructure offers immense opportunities for investors and innovators alike. The country's focus on clean technology, coupled with its commitment to sustainable development, is creating a thriving ecosystem for businesses to grow while addressing environmental challenges.

With strategic global partnerships, robust government support, and a vibrant cleantech ecosystem, India is well on its way to becoming a global leader in renewable energy and sustainability. For investors, the time to engage with this green revolution is now, as the opportunities in clean tech and sustainable infrastructure promise high returns and long-term impact.

ESG Compliance: India's Push for Environmentally Responsible Investments

India is embracing Environmental, Social, and Governance (ESG) principles as a cornerstone of its investment and business landscape, reflecting a global shift toward sustainability and ethical practices. The adoption of ESG not only fosters long-term resilience and accountability in businesses but also attracts international investors eager to align their portfolios with responsible and sustainable initiatives. By integrating ESG into corporate operations, government policies, and financial systems, India is shaping a future where sustainability and economic growth go hand in hand.

Corporate ESG Adoption: Leading the Sustainability Charge

Indian companies are increasingly recognizing the importance of ESG principles as essential to their operations, reflecting a commitment to sustainability, social responsibility, and robust governance.

Reducing Carbon Footprints: Companies across sectors are implementing measures to minimize greenhouse gas emissions, transition to renewable energy, and enhance energy efficiency. For example, IT giants like **Infosys** and **Wipro** have adopted carbon neutrality goals, setting benchmarks for corporate sustainability.

Promoting Social Equity: Beyond environmental considerations, firms are investing in social equity by improving workplace diversity, supporting community development programs, and ensuring fair labor practices. Leading manufacturing and finance companies are incorporating inclusive policies that prioritize workforce well-being and community upliftment.

Sectoral Leadership: Industries such as IT, manufacturing, and finance are spearheading the adoption of ESG principles. In manufacturing, companies are focusing on sustainable supply chains, while financial institutions are incorporating ESG risk assessments into lending and investment decisions. By integrating ESG into their business strategies, Indian companies are not only enhancing their competitive edge but also ensuring long-term profitability and global relevance.

Government Initiatives: Driving Transparency and Accountability

The Indian government is playing a proactive role in encouraging ESG compliance, creating a policy environment that prioritizes sustainability and accountability.

Mandatory ESG Disclosures: The Securities and Exchange Board of India (SEBI) has introduced mandatory Business Responsibility and Sustainability Reporting (BRSR) for listed companies. This ensures transparency in ESG-related activities and provides investors with critical insights into corporate sustainability efforts.

Perform, Achieve, and Trade (PAT) Scheme: This market-based mechanism incentivizes industries to reduce energy consumption and improve energy efficiency. Sectors such as cement, steel, and textiles have benefited significantly, reducing emissions while achieving cost savings.

Incentives for Green Practices: Policies such as tax rebates and subsidies for renewable energy adoption, waste management, and sustainable agriculture encourage businesses to adopt ESG-compliant practices. Government-led initiatives are paving the way for widespread ESG adoption, ensuring that both large corporations and small enterprises contribute to sustainable growth.

Investment in Green Bonds: Financing the Green Transition

India has emerged as one of the largest issuers of green bonds among emerging markets, channeling billions of dollars into renewable energy and sustainable infrastructure projects.

Purpose and Impact: Green bonds are financial instruments designed to fund projects with environmental benefits, such as solar parks, wind farms, and energy-efficient buildings. These bonds enable investors to align their portfolios with sustainability goals while enjoying secure returns.

Global and Domestic Participation: Both domestic and international investors, including development banks and private equity firms, are actively investing in India's green bonds. Notable projects funded through green bonds include large-scale solar parks and urban sustainability initiatives under the Smart Cities Mission.

Scaling Green Financing: As demand for sustainable investments grows, India's green bond market is expected to expand further, offering investors diverse opportunities to contribute to the country's environmental goals. Green bonds underscore India's commitment to financing the green transition while reinforcing its position as a global leader in sustainable finance.

Sustainable Financing Ecosystem: Channeling Resources into ESG Projects

India's financial ecosystem is increasingly prioritizing green loans and ESG-compliant projects, reflecting a shift in how capital is allocated.

Banking Sector Initiatives: Banks are launching green loan products tailored for renewable energy, sustainable agriculture, and waste management projects. Institutions like the State Bank of India (SBI) and ICICI Bank are leading the charge, financing solar parks, EV manufacturing, and water conservation projects.

Role of Financial Institutions: Development banks like the **Asian Development Bank (ADB)** and the **Green Climate Fund** are channeling resources into large-scale ESG projects in India, including solar infrastructure and climate-resilient agriculture. Private equity firms and venture capitalists are investing in startups developing clean technology, circular economy solutions, and sustainable supply chains.

Impact on Key Sectors: Renewable energy projects, including wind and solar farms, receive a significant share of sustainable financing. Investments in waste-to-energy plants, water recycling systems, and sustainable urban infrastructure are further driving India's transition to a low-carbon economy. The growing focus on sustainable financing is helping India scale ESG-compliant initiatives while creating a resilient economic model that aligns with global sustainability goals.

In summary, India's push for ESG compliance is redefining its investment landscape, integrating environmental responsibility with economic growth.

Corporate adoption of ESG principles, backed by proactive government policies, is fostering transparency, accountability, and sustainability. Initiatives such as mandatory disclosures, the PAT scheme, and the green bond market are ensuring that businesses and investors prioritize long-term environmental and social impact.

With its sustainable financing ecosystem and increasing global partnerships, India is positioning itself as a leader in ESG-driven growth. For investors, the rise of ESG compliance in India represents an unparalleled opportunity to align financial returns with responsible investment practices, contributing to a more sustainable future.

India's Competitive Edge in Sustainability

India has emerged as a global leader in renewable energy and sustainability, bolstered by a unique blend of supportive policies, international recognition, and economic advantages. These elements provide India with a distinct competitive edge, making it a preferred destination for investments in clean technology, sustainable infrastructure, and environmentally responsible ventures.

Policy Support: A Clear Roadmap for Growth

India's government has played a proactive role in fostering the growth of its renewable energy and sustainability sectors through a range of forward-looking policies and initiatives.

National Solar Mission: Launched under the National Action Plan on Climate Change, the mission aims to achieve 280 GW of solar energy capacity by 2030. It focuses on creating an enabling environment for solar technology adoption, including financial incentives for large-scale solar parks and rooftop installations. Programs like *Kusum* support the use of solar power in agriculture, promoting sustainability in rural areas.

National Electric Mobility Mission (NEMM): This initiative targets the adoption of electric and hybrid vehicles, with the dual goals of reducing dependence on fossil fuels and curbing air pollution. The Faster Adoption and Manufacturing of Hybrid and Electric Vehicles (FAME) scheme under

NEMM provides subsidies for EV manufacturers and buyers, encouraging market growth.

Production Linked Incentive (PLI) Schemes: PLI schemes for renewable energy and advanced battery manufacturing incentivize companies to invest in sustainable technologies. These schemes are helping to create a robust domestic manufacturing ecosystem for solar panels, wind turbines, and EV batteries.

By providing a clear roadmap for growth, these policies ensure that India remains a frontrunner in renewable energy and sustainability.

Global Recognition: Leadership in the International Solar Alliance

India's commitment to renewable energy has garnered global recognition, cementing its role as a key player in the fight against climate change.

International Solar Alliance (ISA): Founded by India in partnership with France, the ISA brings together over 100 countries to promote solar energy adoption. India's leadership in the ISA reflects its commitment to international cooperation in addressing global energy challenges. Through the ISA, India is driving the development of solar projects in underserved regions, including Africa and Southeast Asia, enhancing its influence as a renewable energy leader.

Participation in Global Climate Agreements: India's active role in climate forums, such as the Paris Agreement and COP summits, highlights its dedication to achieving net-zero emissions by 2070. Its renewable energy targets are aligned with global efforts to limit temperature rise, reinforcing India's reputation as a responsible global citizen.

India's international leadership underscores its ability to drive innovation and collaboration in renewable energy on a global scale.

Cost Advantage: Making Sustainability Affordable

India's cost competitiveness is a significant factor in its renewable energy success, attracting domestic and international investments.

Competitive Labor Costs: With a large and skilled workforce, India offers labor costs that are among the lowest globally, reducing the overall cost of renewable energy projects. This advantage enables companies to produce clean technologies such as solar panels and wind turbines at competitive prices, making India an attractive manufacturing hub.

Economies of Scale: India's ability to execute large-scale projects, such as the Bhadla Solar Park and the Pavagada Solar Park, reduces per-unit costs, enhancing the financial viability of renewable energy initiatives. The scale of production in sectors like solar manufacturing and EV batteries allows for lower costs, benefiting both domestic consumers and export markets.

Low Renewable Energy Costs: The levelized cost of solar and wind energy in India is among the lowest in the world, making renewable energy projects highly competitive compared to fossil fuels. Government subsidies and financing support further reduce costs, encouraging widespread adoption.

India's cost advantages not only make sustainability affordable but also ensure that renewable energy adoption scales rapidly across regions.

In summary, India's competitive edge in sustainability is rooted in its visionary policies, global leadership, and cost advantages. By providing a strong policy framework, actively engaging in international renewable energy initiatives, and leveraging its economic strengths, India has positioned itself as a leader in the global energy transition.

As the world moves toward a more sustainable future, India's ability to combine innovation with affordability ensures that it remains a preferred destination for investments in clean energy and sustainability. With a clear vision and unwavering commitment, India is paving the way for a greener and more inclusive global economy.

Conclusion

India's renewable energy and sustainability journey is more than a response to the global call for climate action—it is a strategic initiative aimed at securing long-term economic resilience, energy independence, and environmental stewardship. By leveraging its abundant natural resources, technological advancements, and policy support, India has positioned itself as a global leader in renewable energy. The country's achievements in solar and wind energy and its pioneering efforts in green hydrogen highlight its ability to innovate and adapt to evolving energy needs.

India's renewable energy strategy is intricately tied to its broader goals of sustainable development. Beyond reducing carbon emissions, these initiatives are creating jobs, fostering regional development, and enhancing energy access for millions. The seamless integration of clean energy into its economic and social framework reflects India's holistic approach to sustainability, which balances economic growth with environmental responsibility.

For global investors, India's green magnetism is a compelling opportunity. The country offers a thriving ecosystem for investments in clean technology, sustainable infrastructure, and ESG-compliant ventures. The push for green bonds, expanding markets for electric mobility, and government incentives for renewable energy projects make India one of the most attractive destinations for sustainable investments.

Moreover, India's growing network of international partnerships underscores its commitment to collaborative progress in addressing global energy challenges. Initiatives like the International Solar Alliance and partnerships with leading economies demonstrate India's proactive stance in shaping the global sustainability agenda.

With its ambitious renewable energy targets, forward-looking policies, and a commitment to environmental and social governance, India is poised to redefine what it means to be a green economic powerhouse. The country's leadership in the energy transition serves as a model for other nations, showcasing how sustainability can be a driver of innovation, growth, and global impact.

For stakeholders, the time to engage with India's renewable energy and sustainability sector is now, as the opportunities it offers promise not only high returns but also a meaningful contribution to building a greener, more equitable world. India is not just leading the way; it is setting the standard for a sustainable future.

6. The Healthcare Magnet: Pharmaceuticals and Biotech

"India: Where Innovation Meets Healing on a Global Scale"

India's healthcare sector is a global powerhouse, earning its reputation as the "pharmacy of the world" by providing affordable and life-saving generic drugs to over 200 countries. As a leader in pharmaceuticals, biotechnology, and medical technology (medtech), India is shaping the future of global healthcare. With cutting-edge advancements in medical tourism, hospital chains, and telemedicine, the country is not just meeting healthcare demands—it's setting the standard for accessible, innovative, and transformative healthcare solutions worldwide. For investors and innovators, India offers unparalleled opportunities in a thriving and dynamic healthcare ecosystem.

India as the Pharmacy of the World: Generic Drugs and Global Healthcare Solutions

India has rightfully earned its title as the "pharmacy of the world," playing a crucial role in making affordable, high-quality medicines accessible across the globe. With its dominance in generic drug production, expertise in Active Pharmaceutical Ingredients (APIs), and unmatched contributions to vaccine manufacturing, India is at the forefront of global healthcare solutions.

Generic Drug Production: Providing Affordable Medicines Globally

India is the largest provider of generic medicines in the world, accounting for approximately 20% of global exports by volume.

Industry Leadership: Indian pharmaceutical companies, including **Sun Pharma**, **Dr. Reddy's Laboratories**, and **Cipla**, have set benchmarks in producing cost-effective and high-quality medicines. These companies are known for manufacturing drugs for critical illnesses, such as **HIV/AIDS**,

diabetes, and **cardiovascular diseases**, at prices significantly lower than those in developed markets.

Accessibility and Affordability: By producing generic versions of branded drugs at a fraction of the cost, India ensures access to life-saving medications for millions of people, especially in low- and middle-income countries. This commitment to affordable healthcare has been a cornerstone of India's pharmaceutical strategy.

Compliance with Global Standards: Indian pharmaceutical companies consistently meet the stringent regulatory standards of markets like the **US**, **UK**, and **EU**, with over 1,400 FDA-approved manufacturing facilities—the highest number outside the US.

India's leadership in generic drugs underscores its ability to deliver high-quality solutions at scale, making it indispensable to the global healthcare system.

APIs and Vaccine Manufacturing: Strengthening the Backbone of Global Healthcare

India's pharmaceutical success is bolstered by its expertise in producing Active Pharmaceutical Ingredients (APIs) and vaccines.

API Production: APIs are the core components of pharmaceutical drugs, and India is one of the largest global producers. Indian companies supply APIs to pharmaceutical manufacturers worldwide, ensuring the availability of essential medicines across various therapeutic categories.

The COVID-19 Pandemic Response: India's pharmaceutical and vaccine manufacturing capabilities came to the forefront during the COVID-19 pandemic. The **Serum Institute of India**, the world's largest vaccine manufacturer by volume, played a pivotal role in producing and distributing billions of doses of COVID-19 vaccines to countries worldwide. Indian companies partnered with global organizations like Gavi and the WHO to ensure equitable vaccine distribution under initiatives like **COVAX**, reinforcing India's commitment to global health.

Biological Advancements: India's growing expertise in biologics and biosimilars has further expanded its footprint in global pharmaceutical markets, offering affordable solutions for complex medical conditions like cancer and autoimmune diseases.

Global Reach: Serving the World's Healthcare Needs

Indian pharmaceuticals are exported to over **200 countries**, reaching both regulated and non-regulated markets.

Regulated Markets: Indian drug manufacturers have made significant inroads into highly regulated markets such as the **United States**, **United Kingdom**, and **European Union**, demonstrating their ability to meet rigorous quality and compliance requirements. In the US alone, Indian generics account for approximately **40% of the total market share** by volume.

Emerging Markets: In addition to regulated markets, Indian pharmaceutical companies cater to the healthcare needs of emerging economies in Africa, Latin America, and Southeast Asia, ensuring widespread access to essential medications.

Robust R&D Capabilities: India's pharmaceutical industry is underpinned by strong research and development (R&D) capabilities. Companies are investing heavily in innovation, including developing new drug formulations, improving manufacturing processes, and exploring advanced therapeutic areas like biologics and gene therapies.

Competitive Pricing: India's ability to deliver high-quality medicines at competitive prices makes it an attractive partner for governments, NGOs, and healthcare organizations globally. This cost advantage is particularly critical in addressing public health challenges in developing nations.

India's Strategic Role in Global Healthcare

India's position as the "pharmacy of the world" is not just about manufacturing medicines—it's about enabling access to affordable healthcare solutions and addressing global health challenges.

Economic Impact: The pharmaceutical sector contributes significantly to India's economy, with exports valued at over $25 billion annually and growing steadily.

Social Impact: By supplying affordable medicines and vaccines, India plays a vital role in improving health outcomes and saving lives worldwide.

Future Potential: With its robust manufacturing base, skilled workforce, and focus on innovation, India is poised to lead advancements in areas like personalized medicine, biosimilars, and precision healthcare.

In conclusion, India's reputation as the "pharmacy of the world" reflects its unmatched capabilities in generic drug production, API manufacturing, and vaccine development. By combining affordability, quality, and innovation, India is transforming global healthcare, ensuring that critical medicines reach those who need them most.

For investors and stakeholders, India's pharmaceutical industry offers immense opportunities in a dynamic and impactful sector that continues to shape the future of global health.

Growth in Biotech, Medtech, and Medical Tourism

India's healthcare sector is rapidly diversifying beyond pharmaceuticals, with biotechnology, medical technology (medtech), and medical tourism emerging as significant growth drivers. These areas are transforming the industry, addressing global health challenges, and positioning India as a leader in innovation, technology, and cost-effective healthcare solutions.

Biotech Innovation: Addressing Global Health and Beyond

India's biotechnology sector is among the top 12 globally, with a wide range of applications spanning healthcare, agriculture, and industrial processes. This sector is driving transformative advancements and creating new opportunities for growth and innovation.

Healthcare Applications: India is a global leader in the development of **biosimilars**, which are critical in providing affordable treatments for chronic and life-threatening diseases such as cancer, diabetes, and autoimmune disorders. Innovations in **gene therapies** and **personalized medicine** are reshaping treatment paradigms by offering targeted and effective solutions tailored to individual patient needs.

Key Players in Biotech: **Biocon**, one of India's leading biotech companies, has developed breakthrough biosimilars and novel biologics, significantly reducing treatment costs for critical diseases. The **Serum Institute of India**, the world's largest vaccine manufacturer, has contributed to global health with affordable vaccines for diseases like meningitis, pneumonia, and COVID-19.

Agricultural and Industrial Biotechnology: Biotech innovation extends beyond healthcare, with advancements in genetically modified crops, biofuels, and industrial enzymes driving efficiency and sustainability in agriculture and industrial processes.

India's robust biotech ecosystem, supported by skilled professionals, R&D capabilities, and government incentives, is propelling the sector to new heights.

Medtech Advancements: Redefining Healthcare Delivery

India's medtech industry is witnessing unprecedented growth, fueled by technological advancements and a focus on local manufacturing. The sector is transforming healthcare delivery with innovative solutions that improve diagnosis, treatment, and patient outcomes.

Technological Innovations: Companies are developing **AI-powered diagnostic tools** that enable early detection of diseases, enhancing the chances of successful treatment. **Robotic surgery systems** are being introduced to improve precision and reduce recovery times, while **wearable health devices** monitor real-time health metrics, empowering patients to manage chronic conditions effectively.

Startups Driving Change: Indian startups are at the forefront of medtech innovation, creating cutting-edge solutions in areas like telemedicine, portable diagnostic devices, and smart prosthetics. Companies like **Forus Health** and **Niramai** are leveraging AI and IoT to develop affordable and accessible healthcare technologies.

Local Manufacturing and Government Support: Initiatives like **Make in India** are encouraging domestic production of medical devices, reducing dependency on imports and making high-quality equipment more accessible. The government's focus on promoting medtech parks and providing tax incentives is creating a thriving ecosystem for medtech manufacturing and innovation.

India's medtech advancements are bridging gaps in healthcare delivery, making quality care accessible to all and enhancing its competitiveness in the global market.

Medical Tourism: A Hub for Affordable and Quality Care

India has emerged as a leading destination for medical tourism, attracting patients from around the world with its combination of high-quality healthcare and affordable costs.

World-Class Healthcare Services: India offers state-of-the-art facilities and highly skilled medical professionals, providing top-notch treatment in areas such as **cardiac care**, **orthopedics**, **oncology**, and **transplant surgeries**. Many hospitals, including **Apollo Hospitals** and **Fortis Healthcare**, are internationally accredited, ensuring that global standards of care are met.

Cost Advantage: The cost of medical procedures in India is a fraction of that in developed countries. For example, cardiac bypass surgery in India costs 10-15% of what it does in the US or UK, without compromising on quality.

Comprehensive Care Packages: Medical tourists benefit from end-to-end care, including pre-treatment consultations, medical procedures, post-treatment recovery, and even travel and accommodation services, ensuring a seamless experience.

Economic Contribution: Medical tourism contributes significantly to India's economy, with revenues projected to surpass **$13 billion by 2025**. This growth is further supported by the government's initiatives, such as **e-Medical Visas**, which simplify the process for international patients seeking treatment in India.

India's medical tourism sector exemplifies the country's ability to combine world-class healthcare with affordability, making it a preferred destination for international patients.

India's Unique Position in Healthcare Growth

India's advancements in biotechnology, medtech, and medical tourism underscore its leadership in delivering innovative, cost-effective, and globally impactful healthcare solutions.

Innovation and Expertise: India's biotech and medtech sectors are pushing the boundaries of healthcare innovation, addressing global health challenges with advanced solutions.

Accessibility and Affordability: Medical tourism highlights India's ability to offer high-quality healthcare services at costs that are accessible to a global audience.

Supportive Ecosystem: Government initiatives, skilled professionals, and a vibrant startup culture are fostering growth and attracting international investments in these sectors.

In conclusion, India's growth in biotechnology, medtech, and medical tourism demonstrates its evolving healthcare landscape, which now extends far beyond pharmaceuticals. The country's ability to innovate and adapt to changing healthcare demands is cementing its reputation as a global healthcare magnet.

For investors, innovators, and healthcare providers, India offers unparalleled opportunities to participate in a dynamic sector that is reshaping the future of global healthcare.

Opportunities in Hospital Chains and Telemedicine

India's healthcare landscape is rapidly evolving, driven by its growing population, increasing awareness of health issues, and the need for advanced healthcare services. This transformation has created significant opportunities in the expansion of hospital networks and the rapid adoption of telemedicine, reshaping how healthcare is delivered across the country.

Hospital Chains: Expanding to Meet Diverse Healthcare Needs

The demand for quality healthcare services is fueling the growth of hospital chains in India, providing investors with lucrative opportunities to support and expand these networks.

Leading Hospital Chains: Prominent players like **Apollo Hospitals**, **Fortis Healthcare**, and **Max Healthcare** are leading the charge in addressing the growing demand for healthcare services. These chains are continually expanding their footprint, establishing new hospitals in tier-1 and tier-2 cities to cater to a wider population.

Investment-Driven Growth: Private equity and venture capital investments are pouring into hospital networks, driving the development of both multi-specialty and single-specialty hospitals. Single-specialty hospitals focusing on areas like oncology, orthopedics, and fertility are gaining traction due to their specialized care offerings and high patient demand.

Trends Redefining Healthcare Delivery: **Patient-Centric Care**: Hospitals are prioritizing patient experience, focusing on personalized care, shorter wait times, and holistic recovery programs.

Advanced Surgical Procedures: The adoption of minimally invasive surgeries and robotic-assisted procedures is enhancing treatment outcomes and reducing recovery times.

Hospital Digitization: Digital transformation is revolutionizing hospital operations, with technologies like electronic health records (EHR), AI-driven diagnostics, and real-time monitoring systems improving efficiency and patient care.

The growth of hospital chains is not just about adding beds—it's about building integrated healthcare ecosystems that combine technology, expertise, and accessibility to meet the healthcare demands of a diverse and growing population.

Telemedicine Revolution: Bridging the Healthcare Gap

Telemedicine has emerged as a transformative force in India's healthcare sector, addressing accessibility challenges and bringing quality healthcare to even the remotest corners of the country.

Exponential Growth During the Pandemic: The COVID-19 pandemic accelerated the adoption of telemedicine, as lockdowns and physical distancing made in-person consultations difficult. Telemedicine platforms experienced a surge in usage, highlighting their potential to deliver healthcare services efficiently and safely.

Leading Telemedicine Platforms: Platforms like **Practo**, **1mg**, and **Mfine** have revolutionized healthcare delivery by offering:

Online Consultations: Connecting patients with doctors across specialties through video and audio calls.

Medicine Delivery: Enabling doorstep delivery of prescribed medicines, improving access to essential drugs.

Diagnostic Services: Facilitating at-home sample collection and digital reports, reducing the need for physical visits to diagnostic centers.

Government-Led Initiatives: The Indian government has been proactive in integrating telemedicine into public healthcare systems through initiatives like the **eSanjeevani platform**. This teleconsultation service connects patients in rural areas with doctors in urban centers, bridging the urban-rural healthcare divide. The government's focus on digital infrastructure and broadband connectivity in rural areas is further supporting the growth of telemedicine.

Emerging Technologies in Telemedicine: AI-powered chatbots, wearable health devices, and remote patient monitoring systems are enhancing the capabilities of telemedicine platforms. Blockchain technology is being explored to ensure secure and efficient sharing of patient data across platforms.

Telemedicine is not just a convenience; it is a necessity in a country as vast and diverse as India, offering scalable solutions to healthcare accessibility challenges.

The Impact of Hospital Chains and Telemedicine

The combined growth of hospital chains and telemedicine is reshaping India's healthcare ecosystem, creating a hybrid model that blends traditional and digital healthcare delivery.

Accessibility: The expansion of hospital networks ensures that more people in urban and semi-urban areas have access to high-quality healthcare services. Telemedicine bridges gaps in rural and remote regions, bringing essential medical services to underserved populations.

Affordability: Telemedicine reduces healthcare costs by minimizing travel expenses and hospital visits, making healthcare more affordable for patients. The presence of a competitive private hospital sector ensures cost efficiency while maintaining high standards of care.

Efficiency: Digital tools and technologies are improving operational efficiency in hospitals and telemedicine platforms, reducing wait times and enhancing patient outcomes.

In conclusion, India's growing demand for advanced healthcare services has unlocked immense opportunities in the expansion of hospital chains and the adoption of telemedicine. The evolution of hospital networks is ensuring that quality care reaches more people, while telemedicine is democratizing access to healthcare, especially in underserved areas.

For investors and innovators, these developments represent an opportunity to be part of a transformative journey that is redefining healthcare delivery in India. By combining traditional healthcare infrastructure with cutting-edge digital solutions, India is creating a resilient, accessible, and patient-centric healthcare ecosystem for the future.

India's Competitive Advantages in Healthcare

India's healthcare sector stands out on the global stage, driven by a combination of cost efficiency, a highly skilled workforce, robust infrastructure, and supportive government policies. These factors collectively position India as a leading destination for healthcare investments, medical tourism, and innovation.

Cost Efficiency: High-Quality Care at Affordable Prices

India's healthcare sector is renowned for its cost efficiency, making it a preferred choice for patients and businesses alike.

Affordable Treatment Costs: India offers world-class medical treatments at a fraction of the cost compared to developed countries. For instance, complex procedures such as cardiac bypass surgery or joint replacements in India cost 10-20% of what they would in the US or Europe, without compromising quality. Affordable healthcare extends to areas like diagnostics, post-operative care, and specialized treatments, making India an attractive destination for medical tourism.

Pharmaceutical Manufacturing: India's ability to produce cost-effective generic medicines has made it the "pharmacy of the world." The country's competitive pricing is a major driver of its pharmaceutical exports, which serve over 200 countries. Economies of scale and efficient supply chains enable Indian manufacturers to produce high-quality drugs and vaccines at globally competitive rates.

India's cost advantage ensures that healthcare is accessible to a wide audience, reinforcing its role as a global healthcare leader.

Skilled Workforce: The Backbone of Excellence

India boasts one of the largest and most skilled healthcare workforces in the world, contributing to its reputation for high-quality care and innovation.

Highly Qualified Doctors: Indian doctors are globally recognized for their expertise and dedication, with many trained at premier institutions like the All India Institute of Medical Sciences (AIIMS). A significant number of Indian doctors and healthcare professionals also work in leading healthcare systems worldwide, underscoring their global competence.

Researchers and Innovators: India has a robust pool of researchers in fields like biotechnology, pharmaceuticals, and medical devices. These professionals are driving advancements in areas such as gene therapies, biosimilars, and AI-driven diagnostics. Institutions like the Indian Council of Medical Research (ICMR) and partnerships with global organizations further enhance India's research capabilities.

Healthcare Workforce Expansion: India's healthcare workforce is growing rapidly, supported by government initiatives to train nurses, technicians, and paramedics to meet the increasing demand for healthcare services. The depth and breadth of India's skilled workforce are critical to its ability to deliver exceptional healthcare services and drive innovation.

Strong Infrastructure: Supporting Growth and Delivery

India's healthcare infrastructure is expanding rapidly, with significant investments in hospitals, research centers, and biotech parks.

Expanding Hospital Networks: A growing number of multi-specialty and single-specialty hospitals, such as Apollo Hospitals, Fortis Healthcare, and Narayana Health, are enhancing healthcare delivery across urban and rural areas. The rise of telemedicine and digital health platforms is further augmenting infrastructure, ensuring healthcare reaches even the remotest regions.

Research and Development Hubs: India is home to numerous research institutions and biotech parks, which support innovation in pharmaceuticals, biotechnology, and medical devices. These hubs enable collaborations between academia, industry, and government, fostering breakthroughs in healthcare technologies and treatments.

Medtech Manufacturing: Medtech parks and production facilities are driving local manufacturing of medical devices, reducing dependency on imports and making advanced healthcare technology more accessible. India's robust infrastructure underpins its healthcare ecosystem, ensuring efficient service delivery and continuous innovation.

Supportive Policies: Driving Growth and Innovation

The Indian government has implemented a range of policies to foster growth, attract investments, and encourage innovation in the healthcare sector.

Ayushman Bharat: Launched as the world's largest government-funded healthcare program, Ayushman Bharat aims to provide free health coverage to over 500 million Indians. This initiative has increased access to quality healthcare services for low-income families while driving demand for healthcare infrastructure and services.

Production Linked Incentive (PLI) Schemes: PLI schemes for pharmaceuticals and medical devices incentivize domestic manufacturing and innovation. These programs aim to reduce import dependency, enhance self-reliance, and position India as a global manufacturing hub for healthcare products.

National Digital Health Mission (NDHM): This initiative aims to create a digital health ecosystem, including a unique health ID for citizens, enabling seamless access to healthcare services and records. NDHM is fostering the adoption of telemedicine, digital health solutions, and AI-driven diagnostics.

Tax Incentives and Regulatory Reforms: The government offers tax benefits and simplified regulatory processes to encourage investments in healthcare infrastructure, R&D, and innovation.State governments are also playing a key role by offering incentives for setting up hospitals and medtech parks.

Supportive policies are enabling India's healthcare sector to grow sustainably while addressing the needs of its population and attracting global partnerships.

In short, India's competitive advantages in healthcare—cost efficiency, a skilled workforce, strong infrastructure, and supportive policies—make it a global healthcare magnet. These strengths not only drive domestic growth but also position India as a key player in addressing global health challenges.

For investors and healthcare innovators, India offers a dynamic and thriving ecosystem with immense potential for growth, innovation, and impact. As the sector continues to evolve, these advantages will play a pivotal role in shaping India's leadership in the global healthcare landscape.

Conclusion

India's healthcare sector is a dynamic and transformative force, standing at the crossroads of innovation, accessibility, and exponential growth. As the "pharmacy of the world," India has established itself as a crucial player in addressing global health challenges through its affordable and high-quality pharmaceutical solutions. From producing life-saving generic medicines to playing a pivotal role in vaccine development and distribution, India's pharmaceutical industry underscores its commitment to global health.

However, India's healthcare story extends far beyond pharmaceuticals. The nation's advancements in biotechnology and medical technology (medtech) are shaping the future of healthcare innovation. Breakthroughs in biosimilars, gene therapies, AI-driven diagnostics, and wearable medical devices are driving a paradigm shift in how healthcare is delivered and experienced. These innovations are not just enhancing the quality of care but also democratizing access to cutting-edge healthcare solutions.

India's healthcare ecosystem is equally defined by its ability to adapt to changing needs. The rise of **medical tourism** showcases the country's capacity to provide world-class care at a fraction of the cost, attracting patients from around the globe for treatments ranging from cardiac surgeries to cosmetic procedures. Similarly, the **telemedicine revolution** has bridged the gap between urban and rural healthcare, ensuring that even the remotest populations have access to medical expertise and services. Meanwhile, the expansion of **private hospital chains** has redefined patient-centric care, integrating advanced surgical techniques and digital innovations to improve outcomes and experiences.

For investors, India's healthcare magnetism offers a unique opportunity to engage with a sector that combines financial returns with meaningful social impact. From pharmaceuticals and biotech to medtech and healthcare delivery, every facet of the industry is ripe for investment, driven by growing demand, strong policy support, and an ever-expanding global market.

India's healthcare sector is more than just an industry—it is a critical enabler of well-being, innovation, and economic growth. As the nation continues to push boundaries and set new standards in healthcare, it reinforces its position as a global leader. For stakeholders, this is not just a chance to participate in a thriving market but to contribute to a transformative journey that blends innovation, accessibility, and social responsibility, solidifying India's role as a beacon of hope and excellence in global healthcare.

7. The Infrastructure Magnet: Building the Future

"India: Where Vision Meets Infrastructure to Shape Tomorrow"

India's infrastructure sector is undergoing a transformative journey, fueled by visionary projects, rapid urbanization, and a steadfast commitment to modernization. From pioneering smart cities to expansive transport corridors like Bharatmala and Sagarmala, the nation is laying the foundation for a future-ready economy. These initiatives are revolutionizing connectivity, urban living, and logistics while unlocking vast opportunities for both domestic and international investors. At the heart of this transformation lies the robust framework of public-private partnerships (PPPs), fostering a dynamic ecosystem that thrives on innovation, operational excellence, and scalable solutions.

Major Projects Transforming India: Smart Cities, Bharatmala, and Sagarmala

India's infrastructure landscape is undergoing a revolutionary transformation, anchored by landmark projects like the Smart Cities Mission, Bharatmala Pariyojana, and Sagarmala Project. These initiatives are redefining urban and rural development, enhancing connectivity, and unlocking economic potential across the nation.

Smart Cities Mission: Creating Future-Ready Urban Spaces

Launched in 2015, the **Smart Cities Mission** is a visionary initiative to develop 100 cities with advanced urban planning, digital integration, and sustainable infrastructure. This project is reshaping the way people live and interact with their cities.

Urban Mobility: Efficient public transport systems, such as metro rail networks and e-mobility solutions, are improving urban commutes. Smart traffic management systems powered by artificial intelligence are easing congestion and optimizing travel times.

Sustainability: Renewable energy adoption in public utilities and residential areas reduces the carbon footprint. Water recycling plants and integrated waste management systems ensure resource conservation and environmental sustainability.

Technology Integration: IoT-enabled services provide real-time monitoring and management of utilities such as electricity, water, and waste. Digital governance platforms enable seamless citizen engagement, simplifying processes like tax payments and service requests.

Cities like **Pune**, **Surat**, and **Bhubaneswar** are leading examples of smart urban living, attracting significant investments in technology, housing, and infrastructure development. These cities showcase how advanced urban planning can improve the quality of life while fostering economic growth.

Bharatmala Pariyojana: Expanding India's Highway Network

The **Bharatmala Pariyojana** is a flagship highway development program designed to strengthen India's road infrastructure and boost economic connectivity. By constructing **34,800 kilometers of national highways**, this initiative is transforming how goods and people move across the country.

Economic Corridors: High-speed corridors are connecting industrial hubs, reducing transit times and logistics costs for businesses. These corridors enhance trade efficiency, making India's exports more competitive in global markets.

Border and Coastal Roads: Roads along India's borders and coastline improve access to remote areas, supporting national security and regional development. These roads also facilitate the movement of goods, particularly in underdeveloped and strategically important regions.

Logistics Parks: Integrated transport and storage facilities, such as logistics parks, are improving supply chain efficiency. These parks reduce overall logistics costs, making Indian industries more competitive on a global scale.

The Bharatmala project is expected to significantly boost trade, reduce transportation costs, and create economic opportunities in remote regions, driving inclusive growth across the country.

Sagarmala Project: Harnessing India's Maritime Potential

The **Sagarmala Project** focuses on port modernization and coastal development, leveraging India's **7,500-kilometer coastline** to transform the country into a maritime hub.

Port Modernization: Ports are being upgraded to handle larger vessels, reduce turnaround times, and accommodate increasing cargo volumes. Advanced technologies and automation are being introduced to enhance operational efficiency at ports.

Port Connectivity: Road, rail, and inland waterway links are being developed to improve access to ports, ensuring seamless movement of goods. Enhanced connectivity reduces logistical bottlenecks, supporting both domestic and international trade.

Coastal Economic Zones (CEZs): Industrial clusters near ports are being established to boost manufacturing and exports. CEZs reduce logistics costs for industries, creating a competitive advantage in sectors like textiles, electronics, and auto components.

By modernizing ports and strengthening coastal infrastructure, the Sagarmala project enhances India's trade competitiveness and promotes regional economic development, particularly in coastal states.

Transformational Impact of These Projects

These transformative infrastructure projects are laying the foundation for India's future economic growth.

Economic Growth: Improved connectivity accelerates industrial development, boosts exports, and attracts foreign investments. Infrastructure development creates millions of jobs, particularly in construction, manufacturing, and logistics.

Sustainability: The focus on renewable energy and sustainable practices in projects like the Smart Cities Mission ensures long-term environmental benefits. Reduced logistics costs and efficient supply chains contribute to more sustainable trade practices.

Global Competitiveness: Advanced infrastructure positions India as an attractive destination for global businesses, strengthening its position in international trade and commerce.

In conclusion, India's infrastructure ambitions, exemplified by the Smart Cities Mission, Bharatmala Pariyojana, and Sagarmala Project, are reshaping the nation's urban and rural landscapes. These initiatives are not just addressing current challenges but are also creating a framework for sustainable and inclusive growth.

For investors and stakeholders, these projects offer a once-in-a-lifetime opportunity to participate in India's growth story, contributing to the creation of world-class infrastructure that supports economic resilience and global competitiveness. Through these transformative efforts, India is building a future that seamlessly blends modernization with tradition, innovation with sustainability, and connectivity with opportunity.

Investment in Urban Development, Transport, and Logistics

India's rapid urbanization, expanding economy, and strategic focus on infrastructure development are creating unparalleled investment opportunities in urban development, transport, and logistics. These sectors are at the core of India's transformation into a globally competitive and future-ready economy.

Urban Development: Building Resilient Cities

The increasing demand for urban housing, commercial spaces, and essential utilities is driving significant investments in urban development projects.

Real Estate and Housing: Urbanization has led to a surge in the demand for residential and commercial properties. Initiatives like the **Affordable Housing Scheme** aim to provide housing for low- and middle-income groups, boosting the construction sector and attracting investment from real estate developers.

Water Supply and Waste Management: Investments in urban water supply systems and integrated waste management are crucial to ensuring sustainable urban living. Technologies like smart water meters and waste-to-energy systems are gaining traction, providing opportunities for technology providers and construction firms.

Flagship Programs Driving Urban Development: **AMRUT (Atal Mission for Rejuvenation and Urban Transformation)** focuses on urban infrastructure upgrades, including water supply, sanitation, and green spaces in 500 cities. Smart Cities Mission projects complement these efforts, creating sustainable and technology-enabled urban ecosystems.

Urban development projects are not just meeting immediate infrastructure needs but are also creating resilient cities equipped for future challenges.

Transport Infrastructure: Revolutionizing Mobility

India's transport infrastructure is undergoing a paradigm shift, with investments in high-speed rail, metro rail, and air connectivity driving modernization and efficiency.

High-Speed Rail: The **Mumbai-Ahmedabad bullet train**, India's first high-speed rail project, is setting the stage for faster and more efficient intercity travel. This project is expected to spur investments in related industries, including rail manufacturing, technology integration, and real estate development along the corridor.

Metro Rail Expansions: Metro rail networks in cities like Bengaluru, Delhi, and Hyderabad are expanding to meet the growing demand for urban mobility. These projects are attracting investments in construction, signaling systems, and rolling stock manufacturing, fostering economic growth in urban centers.

Railways Modernization: Investments in freight corridors, electrification, and station upgrades are enhancing the efficiency and connectivity of India's railway network. Dedicated freight corridors like the **Eastern and Western Corridors** are reducing logistics costs and improving goods movement across regions.

Airports and Regional Connectivity: Under the **UDAN (Ude Desh ka Aam Nagrik)** scheme, regional air connectivity is being expanded to underserved areas, boosting tourism and trade. Investments in new airports, such as the **Noida International Airport**, and upgrades to existing ones are catering to the growing demand for air travel.

India's transport infrastructure development is redefining mobility, creating a seamless and efficient network that supports economic and social growth.

Logistics and Supply Chain: Driving Efficiency and Growth

India's logistics and supply chain sector is witnessing transformative growth, fueled by the rise of e-commerce and the need for streamlined supply chains.

Expanding Logistics Market: The logistics market in India is expected to reach **$380 billion by 2025**, driven by a growing consumer base and increasing trade volumes. This growth is creating investment opportunities in infrastructure such as warehouses, transportation, and supply chain technology.

Warehousing and Cold Storage: The demand for modern warehousing facilities and cold storage systems is surging, particularly in e-commerce, agriculture, and pharmaceuticals. Investments in temperature-controlled storage and automated warehousing solutions are addressing the needs of industries requiring precision and efficiency.

Last-Mile Delivery: With the rapid growth of e-commerce, last-mile delivery is becoming a critical component of the logistics ecosystem. Investments in electric delivery vehicles, drones, and AI-driven route optimization are transforming last-mile logistics.

Multimodal Logistics Parks: Integrated transport systems such as multimodal logistics parks are reducing costs and improving efficiency by connecting rail, road, and air transport. These parks are designed to handle large cargo volumes, improve inventory management, and reduce transit times.

India's logistics sector is evolving into a highly efficient and technology-driven ecosystem, offering immense opportunities for investment and innovation.

Key Drivers of Investment in Infrastructure

✓ **E-Commerce Growth**: The rapid expansion of online retail is driving demand for warehousing, cold storage, and delivery infrastructure.

✓ **Urbanization Trends**: Increasing urban population density is pushing investments in housing, transport, and utilities.

✓ **Policy Support**: Government initiatives like the **National Infrastructure Pipeline (NIP)** and production-linked incentive schemes are creating a favorable environment for private and foreign investments.

✓ **Technology Adoption**: The integration of advanced technologies like AI, IoT, and automation in logistics and transport is improving efficiency and attracting global players.

In conclusion, India's investment opportunities in urban development, transport, and logistics are unparalleled, reflecting the country's commitment to building a modern and sustainable infrastructure. Urban housing and utility projects are creating livable cities, transport infrastructure is redefining mobility, and the logistics sector is emerging as a critical driver of economic growth.

For investors, these sectors offer a chance to engage with transformative projects that not only promise significant returns but also contribute to India's growth story. By capitalizing on these opportunities, stakeholders can play a pivotal role in shaping India's journey toward becoming a global infrastructure leader.

Role of Public-Private Partnerships (PPPs)

Public-private partnerships (PPPs) have emerged as a cornerstone of India's infrastructure development strategy, addressing critical gaps, optimizing resources, and mobilizing private sector expertise for large-scale projects. These collaborations blend the strengths of the public and private sectors, driving efficiency, innovation, and sustainability in infrastructure development.

Key PPP Projects: Exemplifying Success

India's success with PPPs is evident in landmark projects that have redefined urban transport and infrastructure standards.

Delhi Metro: A Global Benchmark

The Delhi Metro is a flagship PPP project and a global success story in urban transport. Combining government funding with private sector efficiency, it offers world-class metro services with high operational standards, punctuality, and safety. The PPP model facilitated seamless integration of advanced technology, efficient management, and robust maintenance practices, making it a model for urban mobility globally.

GMR and GVK Airports: Raising the Bar for Aviation

Privately operated airports like **Delhi's Indira Gandhi International Airport (GMR)** and **Mumbai's Chhatrapati Shivaji Maharaj International Airport (GVK)** have set new benchmarks for passenger experience and operational excellence. These airports are known for their world-class infrastructure, efficient logistics, and high-quality services, achieved through innovative approaches in design and management. The success of these PPP-operated airports has inspired similar models for other airports across India, enhancing regional connectivity and global competitiveness.

Government Support for PPPs: Enabling Collaboration

The Indian government has played a proactive role in promoting PPPs, creating a conducive policy environment, and providing financial incentives to encourage private sector participation.

Viability Gap Funding (VGF): The VGF scheme bridges the gap between project costs and potential revenues, making infrastructure projects financially viable for private investors. Sectors like transport, energy, and social infrastructure, including healthcare and education, benefit significantly from this support.

National Infrastructure Pipeline (NIP): The NIP outlines an ambitious **$1.5 trillion investment plan by 2025**, with 39% of projects earmarked for PPP execution. This pipeline focuses on critical infrastructure areas, including highways, railways, ports, airports, and urban development, highlighting the central role of PPPs in India's growth story.

Policy Reforms: Streamlined regulatory processes, tax benefits, and fast-track approvals ensure that PPP projects are implemented efficiently. State governments are also actively adopting PPP frameworks to address local infrastructure needs, expanding the scope and scale of these partnerships.

Advantages of PPPs: Transforming Infrastructure Development

The PPP model offers several key benefits that make it a vital component of India's infrastructure strategy.

Efficiency: The private sector brings expertise in project management, technology integration, and cost optimization, ensuring timely and efficient execution of projects. Projects like the Delhi Metro demonstrate how PPPs can deliver superior operational standards and customer satisfaction.

Risk Sharing: PPPs distribute financial, operational, and regulatory risks between public and private partners, reducing the burden on the government and ensuring long-term project sustainability. This shared responsibility enhances project viability and minimizes financial exposure for both entities.

Innovation: Private sector involvement introduces global best practices, cutting-edge technologies, and innovative solutions to infrastructure projects. For example, GMR and GVK airports have incorporated advanced logistics and passenger management systems, setting new industry benchmarks.

Financial Mobilization: PPPs attract significant investments from domestic and international private players, including banks, equity funds, and institutional investors. These collaborations free up public resources, allowing the government to focus on social and rural development initiatives.

The Expanding Role of PPPs in India's Infrastructure Future

PPPs are increasingly being adopted across diverse sectors, from transport and energy to social infrastructure and digital services:

Highways and Railways: PPPs are driving the development of highways under **Bharatmala Pariyojana** and railway modernization projects, including station upgrades and high-speed rail initiatives.

Renewable Energy: Partnerships are boosting investments in solar parks, wind farms, and green hydrogen projects, accelerating India's transition to clean energy.

Healthcare and Education: PPP models are enabling the construction of hospitals, medical colleges, and skill development centers, addressing critical social needs.

Digital Infrastructure: PPPs are playing a key role in expanding broadband connectivity and setting up data centers, supporting India's digital transformation goals.

In summary, public-private partnerships are reshaping India's infrastructure landscape, delivering projects that combine innovation, efficiency, and global standards. From urban transport systems like the Delhi Metro to aviation hubs and highways, PPPs have proven their ability to transform infrastructure while ensuring financial sustainability.

With strong government support, a favorable policy framework, and the commitment of private players, PPPs are set to play an even larger role in India's future infrastructure development. For investors, policymakers, and stakeholders, PPPs represent a powerful tool to address infrastructure challenges while unlocking significant economic and social value. Through these partnerships, India is building not just infrastructure, but the foundation for a modern, inclusive, and prosperous future.

India's Competitive Advantages in Infrastructure Development

India's infrastructure sector is rapidly emerging as a global hotspot for investments, driven by unique advantages that set it apart in the competitive landscape. These advantages, rooted in geography, demand dynamics, and policy support, make India a compelling destination for infrastructure development.

Strategic Location: A Gateway to Global Trade

India's geographical positioning offers unparalleled advantages for trade, logistics, and connectivity.

Crossroads of Asia: Situated at the intersection of major trade routes, India serves as a vital link between the East and the West.

Its proximity to key markets in South Asia, Southeast Asia, the Middle East, and Africa positions it as a natural hub for global trade and commerce.

Maritime Potential: With a **7,500-kilometer-long coastline**, India has access to strategic sea lanes, making it a key player in maritime trade.

Ports under the **Sagarmala Project** are transforming India into a global maritime hub, attracting investments in port infrastructure, logistics, and coastal economic zones.

Regional Connectivity: India's infrastructure projects, such as road corridors and rail networks, enhance connectivity with neighboring countries, fostering regional trade and cooperation.

Cross-border initiatives like the **India-Myanmar-Thailand Trilateral Highway** and partnerships with SAARC nations underscore its role in facilitating regional growth.

India's strategic location amplifies its importance in global trade networks, creating opportunities for infrastructure investments that capitalize on its logistical and economic advantages.

Growing Demand: The Infrastructure Imperative

India's rapid urbanization and industrial expansion are driving an insatiable demand for infrastructure development.

Urbanization Trends: India's urban population is projected to grow from **35% in 2021 to 40% by 2030**, adding millions of people to cities each year. This growth fuels demand for urban housing, public utilities, transportation systems, and waste management solutions, creating opportunities for real estate developers, construction firms, and technology providers.

Industrial Growth: Sectors like manufacturing, e-commerce, and renewable energy are expanding rapidly, requiring robust infrastructure support in the form of industrial parks, logistics hubs, and transport networks. Initiatives like **Bharatmala Pariyojana** and **Dedicated Freight Corridors (DFCs)** are designed to meet these needs, reducing logistics costs and enhancing efficiency.

Consumer-Driven Infrastructure: The rise of a middle-class population with increasing disposable incomes is driving investments in retail spaces, commercial infrastructure, and entertainment facilities. E-commerce growth is spurring demand for warehousing, cold storage, and last-mile delivery solutions.

India's growing infrastructure demand is not just a response to current needs—it is a long-term imperative to support the country's economic trajectory and improve quality of life.

Policy Support: Building a Conducive Environment for Investors

India's policy framework is designed to attract and facilitate investments in infrastructure, providing a stable and supportive environment for private and foreign players.

Make in India: This flagship initiative promotes domestic manufacturing and infrastructure development, encouraging investments in industrial parks, smart cities, and transport networks. Policies under Make in India offer tax incentives, streamlined approvals, and financial support for infrastructure projects.

Digital India: Aimed at transforming India into a digitally empowered society, this program supports investments in broadband infrastructure, data centers, and smart utilities. The integration of technology in urban planning, transport, and utilities creates opportunities for tech-driven infrastructure solutions.

State-Level Policies: State governments are implementing infrastructure-focused policies tailored to regional needs, such as industrial corridors, logistics hubs, and renewable energy parks. States like Maharashtra, Tamil Nadu, and Gujarat are leading in attracting investments through investor-friendly policies and partnerships.

National Infrastructure Pipeline (NIP): The NIP, with an investment target of **$1.5 trillion by 2025**, underscores the government's commitment to infrastructure development. It prioritizes projects in transportation, energy, urban development, and logistics, creating a roadmap for public and private sector participation.

India's policy ecosystem provides clarity, incentives, and a streamlined approach, making it an attractive destination for infrastructure investments.

India's Holistic Approach to Infrastructure Development

India's competitive advantages in infrastructure development are further enhanced by its holistic approach:

Integration Across Sectors: Projects like **Smart Cities Mission** and **Bharatmala Pariyojana** demonstrate how urban planning, transport, and logistics are integrated to deliver comprehensive solutions.

Sustainability Focus: Policies promoting renewable energy, green buildings, and waste management ensure that infrastructure development aligns with global sustainability goals.

Global Collaboration: India's strategic partnerships with countries like Japan, the US, and Germany bring in expertise, funding, and technology to elevate infrastructure standards.

In conclusion, India's strategic location, growing infrastructure demand, and supportive policy framework create a fertile ground for investment and innovation. The country's ability to combine geographical advantages, economic momentum, and forward-thinking governance positions it as a global leader in infrastructure development.

For investors and developers, India offers a unique opportunity to be part of a transformative journey, contributing to the creation of world-class infrastructure that supports economic growth, regional connectivity, and global competitiveness. With these advantages, India is not just building infrastructure—it is building the future.

Conclusion

India's ambitious infrastructure development agenda is more than a blueprint; it is a transformative journey that is reshaping the nation's economic and social fabric. Major initiatives like the **Smart Cities Mission**, **Bharatmala Pariyojana**, and **Sagarmala Project** are not just modernizing infrastructure but also redefining how urban and rural areas connect, grow, and thrive. By integrating cutting-edge technology, innovative designs, and sustainable practices, these projects are setting new standards for infrastructure development, enhancing both quality of life and economic productivity.

The **Smart Cities Mission** is pioneering advanced urban solutions, bringing sustainability and technology into the forefront of city planning. With improved urban mobility, efficient resource management, and digital governance, India is creating cities that can support growing populations while fostering economic activity and innovation.

Projects like **Bharatmala Pariyojana** and **Sagarmala** are expanding India's transport and logistics capabilities, bridging the gaps between regions, and enabling faster, more efficient movement of goods and people. These initiatives are not only enhancing domestic trade but also positioning India as a key player in global supply chains.

At the same time, **investments in urban development, transport infrastructure, and logistics** are creating a dynamic ecosystem that aligns with India's vision of a future-ready economy. Integrated transport systems, multimodal logistics parks, and urban rejuvenation projects are laying the groundwork for a modern infrastructure network that meets the demands of a rapidly urbanizing and industrializing nation.

Public-private partnerships (PPPs) stand as the cornerstone of India's infrastructure transformation, combining the strengths of public policy and private sector innovation. Through PPPs, India is mobilizing resources, reducing risks, and delivering high-quality projects at scale. Flagship examples like the **Delhi Metro** and privately managed airports demonstrate how collaboration can lead to world-class infrastructure that sets benchmarks for operational efficiency and passenger experience.

India's infrastructure journey is not without its challenges, but the opportunities far outweigh the obstacles. The country's commitment to integrating **sustainability, technology, and inclusivity** ensures that its infrastructure development is not just about economic growth but also about social progress and environmental stewardship.

For investors, developers, and innovators, India's infrastructure sector offers a wealth of opportunities. The scale of projects, the government's strong policy support, and the growing demand for advanced infrastructure create an unparalleled investment climate. Whether in urban housing, high-speed rail, smart ports, or digital infrastructure, India provides the platform for transformative growth.

As the backbone of its economy continues to evolve, India is reinforcing its position as a **global infrastructure magnet**. With ambitious goals, strategic planning, and a forward-thinking approach, the country is setting benchmarks for **scale, efficiency, and impact** in the global infrastructure arena. For those ready to participate, India's infrastructure sector represents not just a chance to contribute to a nation's progress but also to be part of a journey that is shaping the future of global development.

8. The Agri-Tech Magnet: Revolutionizing Agriculture

"India: Cultivating the Future with Technology and Innovation"

India's agriculture sector is on the brink of a revolution, powered by cutting-edge technology, innovative practices, and strong policy support. The integration of precision agriculture, drones, and IoT is redefining traditional farming, driving productivity, and tackling sustainability challenges head-on. Beyond technological advancements, booming opportunities in food processing, exports, and government-backed agri-tech startups are fostering a dynamic ecosystem that positions India as a global leader in agricultural innovation and transformation.

Innovations in Farming: Precision Agriculture, Drones, and IoT

India's agriculture sector is embracing a technological transformation, with advanced tools and techniques enabling farmers to optimize resources, reduce waste, and boost yields. Innovations like precision agriculture, drones, and IoT are not only revolutionizing traditional farming practices but are also addressing critical challenges such as resource scarcity, environmental sustainability, and climate unpredictability.

Precision Agriculture: Customizing Farming Through Data

Precision agriculture is a game-changer, leveraging data-driven insights to tailor farming practices to specific needs.

Data-Driven Practices: Precision agriculture involves using advanced tools like **GPS-guided tractors**, **soil sensors**, and **satellite imagery** to gather real-time information about soil health, crop conditions, and weather patterns. This data allows farmers to apply fertilizers, water, and pesticides in precise quantities, reducing waste and maximizing efficiency.

Enhanced Productivity: By addressing crop-specific needs, farmers can achieve higher yields and better-quality produce. For example, **soil mapping** identifies nutrient deficiencies, enabling targeted interventions that improve soil fertility over time.

Environmental Impact: Precision farming significantly reduces the overuse of inputs like water and chemicals, mitigating issues like **soil degradation** and **water scarcity**. It promotes sustainable practices that protect biodiversity and reduce carbon emissions.

Precision agriculture is empowering Indian farmers to make informed decisions, enhancing both productivity and profitability while promoting environmental sustainability.

Drones in Agriculture: Eyes in the Sky

Drones are rapidly becoming an indispensable tool in modern farming, offering a cost-effective and efficient way to monitor and manage agricultural activities.

Aerial Surveillance: Drones equipped with **multispectral sensors** provide high-resolution images of fields, allowing farmers to monitor crop health, detect pest infestations, and assess irrigation needs. Early detection of problems enables timely interventions, preventing crop losses and improving overall productivity.

Precision Spraying: Drone spraying technology ensures **uniform application** of fertilizers, pesticides, and herbicides, optimizing resource usage and reducing chemical waste. This method not only lowers labor costs but also minimizes human exposure to harmful chemicals, enhancing safety for farm workers.

Cost-Effectiveness: While drones may represent an initial investment, their ability to cover large areas quickly and efficiently results in long-term cost savings. Their application is particularly valuable in large-scale farming operations and remote areas where manual intervention is time-consuming.

The use of drones is redefining agricultural management, providing farmers with actionable insights and improving operational efficiency.

IoT in Farming: Connecting the Field to the Cloud

The Internet of Things (IoT) is revolutionizing Indian agriculture by integrating smart devices into farming operations, offering real-time insights and automation.

Smart Irrigation Systems: IoT-enabled irrigation systems use **sensors** to monitor soil moisture levels and automate water supply based on crop requirements. This reduces water wastage, especially in water-scarce regions, while ensuring crops receive adequate hydration.

Weather Stations and Forecasting: IoT-enabled weather stations provide hyper-local weather updates, helping farmers anticipate and prepare for adverse conditions like storms or droughts. Predictive analytics derived from IoT data allows farmers to plan sowing and harvesting cycles more effectively.

Automated Greenhouses: IoT solutions enable real-time monitoring and control of temperature, humidity, and lighting in greenhouses, ensuring optimal growing conditions. Automated systems reduce dependency on manual labor and ensure consistency in crop quality.

Risk Mitigation: IoT technology empowers farmers to make informed decisions based on predictive analytics, reducing risks associated with climate variability and pest outbreaks.

IoT is bridging the gap between traditional farming practices and modern technology, enabling data-driven agriculture that enhances both efficiency and resilience.

Transforming Indian Agriculture

The integration of precision agriculture, drones, and IoT is driving a paradigm shift in Indian farming practices. These innovations:

Improve Productivity: By enabling targeted interventions and resource optimization, farmers can achieve higher yields and better returns.

Enhance Sustainability: Advanced technologies reduce resource wastage, minimize environmental impact, and promote long-term agricultural health.

Boost Farmers' Income: Increased efficiency, lower costs, and higher-quality produce directly translate to better earnings for farmers.

Build Resilience: Predictive analytics and real-time monitoring prepare farmers to address uncertainties like climate change and pest infestations effectively.

In conclusion, the adoption of advanced technologies such as precision agriculture, drones, and IoT is revolutionizing Indian farming, blending traditional knowledge with modern innovation. These tools are not only enhancing productivity and sustainability but are also empowering farmers with the insights and resources needed to thrive in an increasingly unpredictable agricultural landscape.

For stakeholders, this wave of innovation represents an exciting opportunity to contribute to India's agricultural transformation, ensuring food security and sustainability for future generations.

Opportunities in Food Processing and Exports

India's agriculture sector, with its vast and diverse production base, provides a solid foundation for the rapidly growing food processing and export industries. These sectors are creating lucrative opportunities for businesses and investors, driving value addition, enhancing job creation, and positioning India as a key player in the global agri-food market.

Food Processing Industry: Adding Value to Agriculture

India's position as one of the world's largest producers of agricultural commodities offers immense potential for growth in the food processing sector.

Abundant Agricultural Production: India leads in the production of fruits, vegetables, grains, and dairy, creating a robust supply chain for the food processing industry. Commodities like mangoes, bananas, milk, wheat, and sugarcane provide raw materials for producing packaged and processed foods.

Rising Consumer Demand: Domestically, changing lifestyles and urbanization are driving demand for packaged, processed, and ready-to-consume foods. Internationally, Indian processed foods are gaining traction due to their quality, variety, and competitive pricing.

Growth Areas:

Cold Storage: Investments in modern cold storage facilities are critical for preserving perishable goods and reducing post-harvest losses.

Supply Chain Infrastructure: Efficient logistics and storage networks are enhancing the movement of raw materials and finished products, ensuring quality and timely delivery.

Value-Added Processing: Opportunities abound in converting raw agricultural products into high-value goods like juices, frozen foods, ready meals, and nutritional supplements.

The food processing industry not only increases the shelf life and value of agricultural produce but also supports farmers by creating consistent demand and reducing seasonal price volatility.

Export Potential: Bringing Indian Agriculture to the World

India's agricultural exports are a significant contributor to the global food market, with Indian products renowned for their quality and affordability.

Key Export Commodities: Products like **spices, basmati rice, tea, coffee, and organic produce** enjoy strong demand in international markets. Spices such as turmeric, cumin, and cardamom are highly sought after for their unique flavors and medicinal properties. India's tea and coffee are recognized globally for their distinct taste and quality, catering to premium markets.

Competitive Advantages: **Pricing**: India's ability to offer competitive prices while maintaining quality gives it an edge in global markets.

Quality Standards: Compliance with international certifications and quality benchmarks ensures widespread acceptance of Indian agricultural exports.

Strategic Location: India's proximity to the Middle East, Southeast Asia, and Africa makes it a natural hub for exporting agricultural goods.

Sustainable Farming: The adoption of organic and sustainable farming practices is opening new markets for premium products, particularly in Europe and North America. Niche markets for organic spices, grains, and fruits are growing, driven by consumer preferences for healthier and environmentally friendly products.

India's agricultural exports not only contribute to foreign exchange earnings but also enhance its reputation as a reliable global supplier of high-quality food products.

Processed Food Exports: Capturing Global Trends

The global appetite for convenience foods has created a burgeoning market for processed Indian food products.

Ready-to-Eat (RTE) and Ready-to-Cook (RTC) Products: Indian RTE and RTC products are gaining popularity in international markets, catering to the demand for convenient and flavorful options. Products like instant curries, frozen parathas, and masala mixes are expanding their reach among global consumers, particularly in the US, UK, and Middle East.

Prominent Indian Brands: Leading Indian brands such as **ITC, Parle, and Amul** are capitalizing on this trend by expanding their portfolios and global presence. These companies are leveraging their strong domestic brand reputation to build trust and loyalty among international consumers.

Export Growth Drivers: Enhanced packaging technologies, extended shelf life, and adherence to international food safety standards are enabling Indian processed foods to penetrate global markets. Collaborations with international retailers and e-commerce platforms are further boosting accessibility and reach.

The processed food sector is not just about meeting consumer demand but also about showcasing India's culinary heritage and innovation to the world.

Transforming Potential into Economic Growth

India's food processing and export sectors offer immense potential for creating value, boosting incomes, and driving economic development.

Job Creation: These sectors are labor-intensive, generating employment opportunities across farming, processing, logistics, and retail. They also empower women and rural communities by providing jobs in food processing units and packaging facilities.

Economic Contribution: Increased food processing and exports contribute to higher GDP growth and foreign exchange reserves. These industries also reduce post-harvest losses, ensuring that a larger share of agricultural produce is utilized effectively.

Investment Opportunities: With government support and rising global demand, the food processing and export sectors present lucrative investment opportunities for businesses, startups, and international players.

In summary, India's vast agricultural base, combined with advancements in food processing and export capabilities, positions the country as a global leader in the agri-food industry. With its competitive pricing, adherence to quality standards, and innovative product offerings, India is not just feeding the world but also redefining how agricultural value is created and delivered.

For businesses and investors, this dynamic ecosystem offers unparalleled opportunities to contribute to India's growth story while tapping into a booming global market. By capitalizing on these trends, stakeholders can help drive India's transformation into a powerhouse of processed foods and agricultural exports, shaping the future of global food supply chains.

Government Policies Supporting Agri-Tech Startups

Recognizing the transformative potential of technology in agriculture, the Indian government has implemented a series of progressive policies and initiatives to nurture the growth of agri-tech startups. These measures aim to foster innovation, improve farm productivity, and modernize Indian agriculture, creating a supportive ecosystem for entrepreneurs and investors alike.

Startup India Program: A Catalyst for Agri-Tech Innovation

The **Startup India initiative** is a flagship program designed to provide a nurturing environment for startups across various sectors, including agriculture.

Financial Incentives and Tax Exemptions: Agri-tech startups benefit from tax holidays, funding support, and access to seed capital under this initiative. Financial incentives encourage the development of technologies that address critical agricultural challenges, such as soil health, irrigation efficiency, and market access.

Collaborative Ecosystem: The program fosters collaboration between startups, research institutions, and farmers, accelerating the adoption of innovative technologies. Initiatives like **incubation centers** and **innovation hubs** provide startups with mentorship, technical expertise, and networking opportunities.

Impact: The Startup India program has catalyzed the growth of agri-tech ventures, enabling them to introduce solutions like AI-powered crop monitoring, IoT-enabled irrigation systems, and blockchain-based supply chain management.

Pradhan Mantri Krishi Sinchayee Yojana (PMKSY): Promoting Efficient Water Use

Efficient water management is a critical need in Indian agriculture, and **PMKSY** addresses this through targeted policies and incentives.

Opportunities for Startups: Startups offering innovative irrigation technologies, such as **drip irrigation systems**, **smart sprinklers**, and **water-saving sensors**, find ample opportunities under this scheme. PMKSY supports projects that integrate water management solutions into smallholder farms, improving resource utilization and productivity.

Impact on Agriculture: The program has significantly improved water-use efficiency, reducing wastage and enhancing crop yields, particularly in arid and semi-arid regions.

Agri-Export Policy: Unlocking Global Markets

The government's **Agri-Export Policy** is a strategic initiative aimed at doubling farmers' incomes by boosting agricultural exports.

Export-Oriented Growth: The policy encourages the export of high-value products such as organic produce, spices, and processed foods, creating opportunities for startups in quality assurance and supply chain optimization. Agri-tech startups play a vital role in ensuring product traceability, meeting global quality standards, and streamlining export logistics.

Support for Export Infrastructure: Investments in cold storage, logistics hubs, and digital platforms under the policy enable startups to facilitate seamless exports, connecting farmers to international markets.

Sustainability and Niche Markets: The rise of organic and sustainable farming practices, supported by agri-tech startups, aligns with the policy's focus on premium global markets.

Digital Agriculture Mission 2021–2025: Advancing Tech-Driven Farming

The **Digital Agriculture Mission** underscores the government's commitment to integrating technology into Indian agriculture.

Focus on Advanced Technologies: The mission promotes the use of **AI**, **blockchain**, **IoT**, and **big data analytics** in farming. Startups are encouraged to develop solutions that enhance precision agriculture, optimize resource use, and enable predictive analytics for better decision-making.

Funding and Mentorship: The mission provides financial support and mentorship for startups working on farm management systems, weather forecasting tools, and market intelligence platforms. Partnerships with private players and research institutions further enhance the reach and impact of digital solutions.

Outcome: By leveraging digital tools, farmers gain access to timely information, efficient farm management systems, and better market connectivity, improving profitability and resilience.

Krishi Vigyan Kendras (KVKs): Bridging Innovation and Implementation

Krishi Vigyan Kendras (KVKs) serve as vital links between research institutions, agri-tech startups, and farmers.

Testing and Deployment: KVKs help startups test their solutions in real-world conditions, ensuring practicality and scalability before broader implementation. These centers provide critical feedback to startups, enabling them to refine their technologies for better adoption.

Farmer Outreach: KVKs act as demonstration hubs, showcasing new technologies to farmers and encouraging adoption through training programs and workshops. By fostering farmer-startup interaction, KVKs accelerate the penetration of innovative solutions into rural areas.

Support for Regional Needs: Each KVK addresses the specific needs of its region, allowing startups to tailor their solutions to local challenges such as water scarcity, pest infestations, or soil degradation.

A Vibrant Ecosystem for Agri-Tech Startups

The Indian government's proactive approach to supporting agri-tech startups is creating a vibrant ecosystem characterized by innovation, collaboration, and growth. Key outcomes include:

Increased Efficiency: Technologies developed by startups are enhancing productivity and resource management in farming.

Enhanced Market Access: Startups are bridging the gap between farmers and markets, reducing inefficiencies in supply chains.

Boosted Farmer Incomes: Through technology adoption and market linkages, startups are helping farmers achieve better prices and profitability.

Sustainability: Solutions focused on water efficiency, organic farming, and reduced chemical use align with global sustainability goals.

In conclusion, India's government-backed initiatives are not just supporting the growth of agri-tech startups but are also driving a larger transformation in agriculture. By fostering innovation, ensuring market connectivity, and addressing critical challenges, these policies are empowering startups to reshape the agricultural landscape.

For entrepreneurs and investors, the ecosystem offers immense opportunities to develop and deploy cutting-edge solutions, contributing to the modernization of Indian agriculture while creating a sustainable and profitable future.

India's Competitive Advantages in Agri-Tech

India's position as a global leader in the agri-tech sector is built on a foundation of strategic advantages that enable innovation, growth, and impact. These strengths, encompassing its vast agricultural resources, cost efficiencies, skilled workforce, and policy backing, make India a hub for agri-tech development and deployment.

Large Agricultural Base: A Vast Testing Ground

India's expansive agricultural landscape provides an unparalleled platform for developing and scaling agri-tech solutions.

Extensive Arable Land: With over **150 million hectares of arable land**, India ranks among the top countries in terms of agricultural area, making it ideal for testing and implementing diverse agri-tech innovations. The variety of crops grown across different regions, from wheat and rice in the north to spices and tea in the south, ensures that agri-tech solutions can address a broad spectrum of agricultural needs.

Diverse Climates and Soil Types: India's agro-climatic zones and varied soil types allow for the application of technologies tailored to specific conditions, creating opportunities for precision agriculture and localized solutions. This diversity enables startups to refine and optimize their innovations for global applicability, making India a critical player in the global agri-tech ecosystem.

Cost Advantage: Competitive Edge in Development and Deployment

India's cost structure offers a significant advantage for both the development and deployment of agri-tech solutions.

Affordable Labor: India's large agricultural workforce provides a cost-effective environment for piloting and scaling technologies such as drones, IoT devices, and smart irrigation systems. Low labor costs also make India a preferred destination for global companies looking to manufacture agri-tech tools and equipment.

Low Manufacturing Costs: India's robust manufacturing infrastructure and economies of scale contribute to reduced production costs for agri-tech hardware, such as sensors, drones, and automated machinery. The availability of raw materials and skilled labor further enhances cost efficiency, enabling competitive pricing in both domestic and international markets.

Global Market Appeal: India's ability to deliver high-quality, affordable solutions makes its agri-tech innovations attractive to cost-sensitive markets in Africa, Southeast Asia, and Latin America.

Skilled Workforce: Driving Innovation

India's growing pool of tech-savvy entrepreneurs, agricultural scientists, and skilled professionals is a driving force behind its agri-tech leadership.

Innovative Entrepreneurs: A vibrant startup culture is fueling the development of cutting-edge solutions in precision agriculture, blockchain-based supply chains, and AI-driven farm management. Many entrepreneurs are leveraging India's unique agricultural challenges as opportunities to create scalable and impactful technologies.

Academic and Research Excellence: Institutions like the **Indian Council of Agricultural Research (ICAR)**, **Indian Institutes of Technology (IITs)**, and agricultural universities are producing world-class talent in agri-science and technology. Collaborative research projects between academia and startups are fostering breakthroughs in areas like biosensors, genetics, and sustainable farming practices.

Upskilled Farmers: Increasing awareness and training programs are empowering farmers to adopt and benefit from agri-tech solutions, creating a ready market for innovative tools and systems.

Policy Support: Enabling Growth and Innovation

The Indian government's proactive policies and funding programs provide a strong foundation for the growth of agri-tech startups and investments.

Startup India Initiative: This flagship program offers tax exemptions, financial incentives, and access to funding for agri-tech startups, creating a supportive ecosystem for innovation. It also promotes collaboration between startups, research institutions, and farmers, accelerating the adoption of new technologies.

Digital Agriculture Mission 2021–2025: The mission integrates advanced technologies like AI, blockchain, and IoT into agriculture, encouraging startups to develop digital solutions for farm management and precision agriculture.

Subsidies and Schemes: Subsidies for technologies like drip irrigation, solar pumps, and smart farming equipment lower the barriers for farmers to adopt modern tools. Programs like **Pradhan Mantri Krishi Sinchayee Yojana (PMKSY)** promote efficient water use, opening opportunities for startups in irrigation and water management.

Export-Oriented Policies: The **Agri-Export Policy** focuses on doubling farmers' incomes through export growth, creating opportunities for startups in supply chain optimization, quality assurance, and export facilitation.

Support for Research and Innovation: Government-funded incubation centers and innovation hubs provide resources for startups to test, refine, and scale their solutions.

Collaboration with international organizations and funding agencies expands access to global markets and expertise.

A Unique Combination of Strengths

India's competitive advantages in agri-tech are not just individual strengths—they form a synergistic ecosystem that drives continuous growth and innovation.

Global Impact: India's ability to combine its vast agricultural base with advanced technology positions it as a leader in addressing global challenges like food security and climate resilience. Innovations developed in India often find relevance in other emerging economies, making it a critical player in the global agri-tech landscape.

Scalable Solutions: The diversity and scale of India's agriculture provide a real-world testing ground for solutions that can be scaled domestically and internationally. Cost-efficient production and deployment ensure that these solutions are accessible to farmers at all economic levels.

Sustainability Focus: The integration of sustainable practices, supported by technology and policy, aligns India's agri-tech growth with global environmental goals.

In summary, India's leadership in the agri-tech sector is rooted in its unique competitive advantages: a vast and diverse agricultural base, cost efficiencies, a skilled workforce, and supportive government policies. Together, these factors create an environment that fosters innovation, scalability, and impact.

As India continues to leverage these strengths, it solidifies its position as a global hub for agri-tech solutions, offering immense opportunities for investors, entrepreneurs, and stakeholders to contribute to the transformation of agriculture worldwide.

Conclusion

India's agri-tech sector stands as a beacon of transformation, redefining the future of agriculture by harmonizing the strengths of traditional farming practices with the limitless possibilities of modern technology. From the precision of data-driven agriculture to the innovation brought by drones and IoT, India is not just enhancing productivity but also creating a sustainable model that addresses critical global challenges such as resource scarcity, climate resilience, and food security.

A Revolution in Agriculture

The integration of **precision agriculture** has empowered farmers with insights that optimize resource utilization, reduce waste, and maximize yields. Advanced technologies like **drones** are enabling efficient monitoring, pest control, and crop management, while **IoT solutions** provide real-time data for smarter decision-making. These innovations are not just solving immediate challenges but are also laying the groundwork for long-term sustainability in agriculture.

The impact of these technologies extends beyond the fields. **Food processing** and **exports** are unlocking immense value along the supply chain, driving job creation, reducing post-harvest losses, and strengthening India's position as a global leader in the agri-food sector. The surge in demand for processed foods and organic produce in international markets highlights India's ability to deliver quality and competitiveness on a global scale.

A Thriving Ecosystem for Innovation

India's progress in agri-tech is fueled by an ecosystem that thrives on innovation and collaboration:

Government policies like the Startup India program and Digital Agriculture Mission provide financial incentives, funding support, and mentorship, enabling startups to scale their operations.

Research institutions and Krishi Vigyan Kendras (KVKs) act as bridges between technological advancements and on-ground implementation, ensuring that solutions are practical and impactful.

A **skilled workforce** of agricultural scientists, tech-savvy entrepreneurs, and forward-thinking policymakers contributes to a vibrant ecosystem that continuously pushes boundaries.

This supportive framework ensures that innovations reach farmers, transforming agriculture from a traditionally resource-intensive sector into a modern, technology-driven powerhouse.

Opportunities for Investors and Entrepreneurs

India's agri-tech magnetism is a compelling call for investors and entrepreneurs to participate in a sector poised for exponential growth.

Investors: With vast opportunities in precision farming tools, food processing infrastructure, and export-driven supply chains, India offers a high-potential market for sustainable returns.

Entrepreneurs: Startups have the chance to tackle pressing challenges such as water scarcity, soil health, and market access, creating scalable solutions that benefit both farmers and consumers.

The global relevance of India's agri-tech solutions also opens avenues for international collaboration, with technologies and practices developed here finding applications in other emerging markets across Africa, Asia, and Latin America.

Shaping the Future of Farming

India's leadership in agri-tech is not merely a response to domestic challenges—it is a vision for a global agricultural renaissance. As the world grapples with issues of food security and environmental sustainability, India's agri-tech innovations present a scalable and impactful blueprint for the future.

The sector's journey is marked by resilience, innovation, and an unyielding commitment to progress. By blending traditional wisdom with technological advancements, India is not only transforming its own agricultural landscape but also contributing to a more sustainable and prosperous world.

The Path Ahead

India's agri-tech sector is more than a success story—it is a movement that holds the promise of reshaping agriculture for generations to come. For stakeholders willing to invest in this journey, the rewards extend beyond financial returns to the fulfillment of playing a part in solving one of humanity's most critical challenges: feeding a growing global population sustainably.

As India continues to lead this transformation, its agri-tech magnetism will serve as a cornerstone for a future where technology and tradition coalesce to ensure food security, economic growth, and environmental harmony. The opportunities are vast, and the potential is limitless—India's agri-tech revolution is just beginning.

9. The Consumer Magnet: India's Growing Middle Class

"India's Middle Class: The Billion-Dollar Force Reshaping Global Markets"

India's burgeoning middle class is a game-changer, transforming the nation into a consumer powerhouse and driving exponential growth across sectors like retail, fast-moving consumer goods (FMCG), and e-commerce. With rising incomes, shifting consumption patterns, and a growing appetite for global brands, this demographic evolution represents a golden opportunity for businesses and investors worldwide. This chapter explores the rise of India's middle class, the vast opportunities it offers, and how global brands are adapting to thrive in this vibrant and dynamic market.

Rise of India's Middle Class and Its Impact on Consumption Patterns

India's middle class is more than a growing demographic; it is the engine driving the nation's economic transformation. This burgeoning segment is reshaping consumption trends, influencing market dynamics, and creating unprecedented opportunities for businesses across various sectors.

Demographic Transformation: A Middle-Class Surge

Rapid Growth: India's population of over **1.4 billion** includes a middle class projected to expand to **700 million people by 2030**, accounting for nearly half the nation's population.

This growth positions India as one of the largest consumer markets in the world, attracting global and domestic businesses seeking to tap into this demographic dividend.

Rising Incomes and Education: Improved **educational attainment** and access to better employment opportunities are elevating disposable incomes, shifting the focus from necessity-based spending to aspirational consumption. The rise in dual-income households, particularly in urban areas, is further boosting purchasing power.

Urbanization Trends: Increasing urban migration is concentrating middle-class populations in cities, fostering demand for modern housing, transportation, and urban amenities. Urban centers are becoming hotspots for retail, FMCG, and e-commerce growth, with localized trends influencing broader consumption patterns.

The demographic transformation of India's middle class is creating a powerful consumer base that influences not only domestic markets but also global trade and investment strategies.

Evolving Consumption Patterns: Aspiration Meets Affordability

Aspirational Consumption: India's middle class is moving beyond essentials to embrace products and services that enhance quality of life and reflect personal aspirations. Categories like **electronics**, **fashion**, **personal care**, and **wellness** are witnessing explosive growth, with consumers willing to pay a premium for better experiences and advanced features. Luxury items, once considered unattainable, are becoming increasingly accessible, with brands introducing mid-range options to cater to aspirational buyers.

Convenience-Driven Demand: Changing lifestyles are driving demand for **ready-to-eat foods**, **home delivery services**, and **tech-enabled solutions**, particularly among urban and young consumers. The adoption of digital platforms for grocery shopping, meal delivery, and online learning reflects a shift towards convenience as a key driver of consumption.

Focus on Health and Sustainability: Health-conscious consumers are fueling demand for organic foods, fitness equipment, and wellness products, creating new markets for FMCG and health-tech startups. A growing awareness of environmental issues is driving interest in eco-friendly products and sustainable practices, influencing purchasing decisions across income brackets.

The evolving consumption patterns of India's middle class highlight a shift from necessity to lifestyle-driven choices, opening up opportunities for innovation and brand differentiation.

Rural Middle Class Growth: The Silent Revolution

India's middle class is not confined to urban areas; **rural India** is playing a pivotal role in this transformation, contributing significantly to national consumption trends.

Education and Technology: Expanding access to education and affordable technology is empowering rural populations to improve their earning potential and participate in the consumption economy. Government programs aimed at enhancing rural education, health, and livelihoods are further elevating disposable incomes in these areas.

Digital Penetration: The availability of **affordable smartphones** and **low-cost internet access** is bridging the urban-rural divide, enabling rural consumers to explore e-commerce, digital payments, and online services. Platforms like **JioMart** and **Meesho** are tapping into rural markets, offering products tailored to local needs and preferences.

Infrastructure Development: Improved connectivity through roads, railways, and digital networks is facilitating the delivery of goods and services to remote areas, enhancing market access for businesses. The rise of micro-entrepreneurship in rural India, supported by government and private initiatives, is creating localized demand for consumer goods and services.

Rural India's growing middle class is an untapped goldmine, contributing to the broader narrative of consumption-driven growth while redefining traditional market boundaries.

Impact on Economic Contribution

The rise of India's middle class is not merely a demographic shift; it is a transformation in **economic behavior, aspirations, and market influence**.

Increased Spending Power: The middle class contributes significantly to GDP growth through sustained demand for goods and services. Their spending patterns influence manufacturing, retail, FMCG, and technology sectors, creating a multiplier effect on the economy.

Driving Entrepreneurship: The rise of middle-class entrepreneurs is fostering innovation and expanding economic activity in both urban and rural areas. Businesses catering to this demographic are evolving to provide localized solutions, creating jobs and boosting local economies.

Global Impact: The middle class's preference for international brands and premium experiences is attracting global companies to invest in India, creating cross-border trade and cultural exchange opportunities. Indian consumers are shaping trends in global e-commerce, with companies adapting products and strategies to cater to this influential market.

In conclusion, the rise of India's middle class is more than just a story of economic growth; it is a narrative of empowerment, aspiration, and transformation. This demographic shift is redefining consumption patterns, driving innovation, and reshaping the country's economic landscape.

For businesses and investors, the burgeoning middle class represents a golden opportunity to tap into one of the most dynamic and diverse consumer markets in the world. As this segment continues to grow and evolve, it will remain a cornerstone of India's economic story, setting the stage for a future defined by prosperity, innovation, and global influence.

Opportunities in Retail, FMCG, and E-Commerce

India's burgeoning middle class is fueling exponential growth in three key sectors: retail, FMCG (fast-moving consumer goods), and e-commerce. Each of these sectors is undergoing rapid transformation, offering unique opportunities for businesses and investors to tap into a diverse and expanding consumer base.

Retail: Modernizing Shopping Experiences

India's retail sector is evolving to meet the demands of a younger, more aspirational middle class.

Modern Retail Formats: The proliferation of **malls, supermarkets, and branded retail outlets** is reshaping the shopping experience, blending convenience with a premium feel. Retail giants like Reliance Retail, Tata's Trent, and D-Mart are leading the charge, offering curated selections across categories like apparel, groceries, and electronics. Shopping malls are becoming lifestyle hubs, integrating retail, dining, and entertainment to attract urban and semi-urban consumers.

Omnichannel Approach: Retailers are increasingly adopting an **omnichannel strategy**, merging online and offline platforms to deliver seamless customer experiences. Consumers now enjoy options like browsing online and picking up in-store or using virtual assistants to enhance their shopping experience. Brands like Zara and Decathlon have successfully implemented omnichannel models, strengthening customer loyalty and engagement.

Regional and Local Markets: **Tier 2 and Tier 3 cities** are emerging as new growth frontiers, driven by rising incomes and improved infrastructure. Retailers are tailoring their offerings to regional preferences, from ethnic wear to locally sourced products.

This localization not only boosts sales but also deepens connections with consumers in these expanding markets.

FMCG: A Booming Consumer Goods Sector

The FMCG sector is riding a wave of growth, supported by increasing incomes, changing lifestyles, and heightened consumer awareness.

Health and Wellness: The growing focus on health and wellness is driving demand for **organic, natural, and clean-label products** in categories like food, beverages, and personal care. Brands like Patanjali, Dabur, and Himalaya are thriving by offering products that resonate with health-conscious consumers.

Premiumization: Middle-class consumers are increasingly willing to pay a **premium for quality and branded goods**, fueling growth in segments like skincare, high-end beverages, and gourmet foods. Global FMCG players like Nestlé, Unilever, and Procter & Gamble are introducing premium product lines to cater to this demand.

Rural FMCG: Rural India's growing middle class is becoming a significant contributor to FMCG growth. Companies are **leveraging extensive distribution networks** to ensure product availability in remote areas, tailoring offerings to rural preferences and price points. Packaged goods like biscuits, snacks, and small-sized personal care products are particularly popular in rural markets.

The FMCG sector's ability to cater to diverse demographics—rural and urban, mass-market and premium—positions it as a cornerstone of India's consumer economy.

E-Commerce: Revolutionizing the Consumer Landscape

India's e-commerce sector is one of the fastest-growing in the world, driven by digital penetration and changing shopping behaviors.

Market Growth: The e-commerce market in India is expected to grow to **$200 billion by 2027**, supported by smartphone adoption, affordable data plans, and increasing internet access.

Online Marketplaces: Platforms like **Amazon**, **Flipkart**, and **Meesho** are enabling consumers to access a wide range of products, from essentials to luxury goods. These platforms offer localized interfaces, multilingual support, and hyper-local delivery options, making them accessible to first-time digital shoppers.

Direct-to-Consumer (D2C) Brands: Startups and legacy companies are launching **D2C channels**, bypassing traditional intermediaries to directly connect with consumers. Brands like Boat, Mamaearth, and Lenskart have achieved remarkable success by offering niche, personalized products through their own digital platforms.

Last-Mile Delivery: Innovations in logistics and delivery are bridging gaps in access, making e-commerce feasible even in remote areas. Companies like Delhivery and Ecom Express are enhancing supply chain efficiency, while initiatives like **Amazon's Project Udaan** focus on rural e-commerce penetration. E-commerce is not just about convenience—it is reshaping how Indians shop, bridging the urban-rural divide, and creating new opportunities for small and large businesses alike.

The Convergence of Retail, FMCG, and E-Commerce

The interplay between these three sectors is creating a **dynamic consumer ecosystem**:

✓ **Retail Meets E-Commerce**: Omnichannel strategies are blending the physical and digital, offering consumers the best of both worlds.

✓ **FMCG Goes Digital**: E-commerce platforms are enabling FMCG brands to reach wider audiences, with online grocery platforms like BigBasket and Blinkit driving growth.

✓ **Rural Penetration**: Companies are leveraging both physical retail and digital platforms to cater to the rural middle class, ensuring access to quality products and services.

In conclusion, India's middle class is at the heart of the growth story in retail, FMCG, and e-commerce. As these sectors evolve to meet changing consumer preferences, they offer immense opportunities for businesses and investors to innovate, expand, and thrive. The convergence of these industries is shaping a future where convenience, quality, and accessibility define the Indian consumer experience, solidifying the country's status as a global consumer magnet.

The Role of Global Brands Entering India's Market

India's growing middle class, characterized by rising incomes and aspirational consumption, offers a fertile ground for global brands to expand their presence. The dynamic nature of this market encourages innovation, adaptation, and collaboration, making India an indispensable part of global growth strategies.

Understanding Local Preferences: The Key to Success

Global brands entering India recognize that adapting to local tastes and cultural nuances is critical to capturing consumer loyalty.

Tailoring Offerings: Brands like **McDonald's** and **Domino's** have localized their menus to cater to Indian palates, introducing items such as the **McAloo Tikki Burger** and **Paneer Pizza**. Similarly, **Starbucks** offers regionally inspired flavors like **filter coffee** and **masala chai** to appeal to Indian consumers.

Cultural Sensitivity: Global brands invest in understanding Indian festivals, traditions, and values, incorporating these elements into marketing campaigns and product launches. For example, **Nike** has released collections inspired by Indian art and culture, resonating with local buyers.

Regional Customization: Recognizing the diversity of India, brands often create region-specific offerings, catering to unique preferences and consumption habits in different states. By embracing India's rich cultural diversity, global brands can build deep connections with their target audience, fostering long-term loyalty.

Collaborations and Partnerships: Navigating the Market

Entering a complex market like India often requires strategic partnerships with local entities to ensure smooth operations and market acceptance.

Leveraging Local Expertise: Collaborating with Indian businesses helps global brands navigate **regulatory environments**, streamline supply chains, and establish distribution networks. For instance, **IKEA** partnered with local vendors to source materials, aligning its product offerings with Indian needs while meeting sustainability goals.

Joint Ventures: Global brands often enter the market through joint ventures to share risks and gain local insights. **Hyundai**'s partnership with Indian suppliers has played a crucial role in its dominance in the Indian automotive market.

Building Trust: Partnerships with trusted local entities enhance brand credibility, especially in rural and semi-urban areas where international names may initially lack recognition.

Collaborations not only ease market entry but also enable global brands to integrate seamlessly into India's unique economic and cultural landscape.

Expanding Affordability: Balancing Price and Aspiration

India's middle class is diverse, encompassing consumers with varying spending capacities. Global brands are adopting innovative strategies to cater to both value-driven and premium segments.

Budget-Friendly Offerings: Recognizing the price sensitivity of many Indian consumers, brands like **Xiaomi** and **Samsung** have introduced affordable product lines while maintaining high-quality standards. Apparel brands like **H&M** and **Uniqlo** have launched collections at competitive prices to appeal to cost-conscious buyers.

Premium Aspirations: Alongside budget-friendly options, global brands are retaining their premium offerings to attract aspirational consumers willing to spend on luxury. For example, **Apple** has expanded its footprint in India by introducing financing options for its premium devices, making them accessible to a broader audience.

Localized Marketing: Promotional strategies highlighting affordability without compromising on quality resonate strongly with Indian consumers, who seek value in every purchase.

By balancing affordability with premium aspirations, global brands are successfully addressing the diverse needs of India's middle class.

Sustainability and Responsibility: Winning Hearts with Values

India's middle class is becoming increasingly aware of environmental and social issues, compelling global brands to adopt responsible business practices.

Eco-Friendly Practices: Many brands are introducing **sustainable packaging** and using **renewable energy** in their operations to align with consumer preferences for eco-conscious products. **Unilever** and **Coca-Cola** are investing in sustainability initiatives to reduce their carbon footprints and ensure ethical sourcing.

Corporate Social Responsibility (CSR): Global brands are engaging in community-building activities, such as funding education programs, supporting rural development, and promoting gender equality. Companies like **Tata Starbucks** focus on empowering women and underprivileged communities as part of their CSR commitments.

Transparency and Accountability: Consumers increasingly value brands that demonstrate ethical practices and social responsibility, prompting global companies to prioritize transparency in their operations.

By adopting sustainable practices and giving back to society, global brands are building goodwill and fostering emotional connections with Indian consumers.

India: A Partner in Innovation for Global Brands

India's middle class is not merely a consumer base—it is a collaborator in shaping global strategies and innovations.

Co-Creation: Global brands are involving Indian consumers in the innovation process, leveraging insights to create products that resonate both locally and globally. For example, **PepsiCo's Kurkure** was developed specifically for Indian tastes and later adapted for other markets.

Global Learnings: The success of tailored strategies in India often provides a blueprint for global markets with similar demographics or cultural dynamics. India's middle class offers global brands an unparalleled opportunity to innovate, expand, and refine their offerings, creating a mutually beneficial relationship that drives growth and impact.

In summary, India's growing middle class presents an unparalleled opportunity for global brands to thrive in one of the world's most dynamic consumer markets. By understanding local preferences, forming strategic partnerships, balancing affordability with premium offerings, and embracing sustainability, global brands are not just entering the Indian market—they are becoming an integral part of its growth story.

As India continues to evolve as a consumer magnet, it offers global brands the chance to co-create innovative products and experiences that resonate locally and inspire globally, solidifying their presence in this vibrant and transformative market.

India's Competitive Advantages for Consumer Markets

India's position as a global consumer magnet is anchored in a combination of demographic strength, digital transformation, supportive policies, and market diversity. These factors create a dynamic environment that caters to businesses across industries and price segments, driving sustained growth and innovation.

Young Population: A Thriving Consumer Base

Demographic Dividend: With a **median age of 28 years**, India is home to one of the youngest populations in the world, translating into a long-term, vibrant consumer base. A large proportion of the population is in the workforce, leading to rising disposable incomes and increased purchasing power.

Youth-Driven Consumption: Young consumers are fueling demand for categories such as fashion, electronics, fitness, and entertainment. This segment is highly aspirational, prioritizing lifestyle products, experiences, and technology-driven solutions.

Adoption of Trends: The younger demographic is quick to embrace new trends, from online shopping and subscription services to fintech and shared mobility platforms, driving innovation in consumer markets.

India's youthful population ensures sustained demand for goods and services, making it a robust and resilient market for long-term growth.

Digital Revolution: Connecting Millions to Markets

India's digital transformation is revolutionizing consumer behavior, enabling businesses to reach previously untapped markets.

Affordable Smartphones and Data: The availability of **low-cost smartphones** and **inexpensive data plans** has brought millions of Indians online, creating a thriving digital ecosystem. Platforms like **YouTube**, **WhatsApp**, and **Instagram** have become integral to how Indians discover, shop, and interact with brands.

E-Commerce Boom: Digital penetration has led to the rapid growth of **e-commerce platforms**, allowing consumers across urban and rural areas to access a wide range of products. The adoption of **digital payments**, facilitated by platforms like UPI, Paytm, and PhonePe, has made transactions seamless and secure.

Tech-Savvy Consumers: Consumers are increasingly leveraging technology for comparison shopping, personalized recommendations, and on-demand services, creating opportunities for brands to innovate. The rise of digital-first brands and **direct-to-consumer** (D2C) models reflects the growing influence of online consumers.

The digital revolution is not just expanding India's consumer market—it is reshaping it, creating opportunities for both traditional businesses and tech-driven startups.

Policy Support: Enabling Consumer-Driven Growth

India's government policies provide a strong foundation for consumer market expansion, fostering innovation, investment, and inclusivity.

Digital India: This initiative aims to transform India into a digitally empowered society, promoting internet access, digital literacy, and e-governance. Digital India has created a supportive ecosystem for businesses to thrive, particularly in e-commerce, fintech, and digital content.

Make in India: Encouraging domestic production, Make in India has boosted local manufacturing in sectors like electronics, apparel, and automobiles. The initiative also supports job creation, contributing to rising incomes and enhanced consumer spending.

Support for Startups: Programs like **Startup India** and sector-specific incentives for MSMEs (Micro, Small, and Medium Enterprises) encourage entrepreneurship, leading to innovative solutions tailored to Indian consumers.

Rural Development Policies: Government schemes focused on rural electrification, road connectivity, and financial inclusion are unlocking new consumer markets in previously underserved areas.

Supportive policies not only fuel growth but also enhance the ease of doing business, attracting both domestic and global players to India's consumer markets.

Diverse Market: Opportunities Across the Spectrum

India's consumer market is uniquely diverse, encompassing a broad range of income levels, preferences, and geographic segments.

Luxury and Premium Segments: Affluent urban consumers are driving demand for **luxury goods** and **high-end services**, from international fashion brands to premium automobiles. Cities like Mumbai, Delhi, and Bengaluru are emerging as hubs for luxury retail, supported by rising disposable incomes and aspirations.

Mass Market Opportunities: India's large lower- and middle-income population ensures sustained demand for **affordable products** in categories like FMCG, clothing, and electronics. Companies are innovating to deliver quality products at competitive prices, catering to value-conscious consumers.

Rural Markets: Rural India represents a vast, untapped market, with increasing penetration of consumer goods and technology. Products tailored for rural affordability and utility, such as small-packaged FMCG items and budget-friendly smartphones, are gaining traction.

Cultural Diversity: India's regional diversity allows businesses to create localized offerings, from ethnic clothing to region-specific food products, ensuring deeper market penetration. This diversity ensures that businesses across price points and categories can find a niche in India, making it one of the most inclusive and expansive consumer markets globally.

In summary, India's consumer market is uniquely positioned to offer sustained growth, driven by its youthful population, digital transformation, supportive policies, and market diversity. These competitive advantages create a dynamic environment where businesses can innovate, scale, and thrive.

As India's consumer magnetism continues to attract global attention, it reinforces its status as a pivotal player in shaping the future of retail, e-commerce, and FMCG sectors worldwide. For businesses and investors, India represents not just a market but a gateway to innovation, inclusivity, and long-term success.

Conclusion

India's burgeoning middle class stands as the driving force behind a consumer revolution that is reshaping the nation's economic landscape. With aspirations fueled by rising disposable incomes and an increasing appetite for quality products and experiences, this demographic is not just a passive participant in the economy—it is actively transforming industries and defining the future of consumption.

A Catalyst for Unprecedented Growth

The middle class's impact is most evident in the exponential growth of sectors like **retail**, **FMCG**, and **e-commerce**, which are witnessing significant evolution to meet the demands of this dynamic consumer base.

Retail is shifting from traditional formats to modern, omnichannel experiences, blending physical stores with digital convenience.

FMCG is rapidly adapting to consumer preferences for health, wellness, and premiumization, while tapping into rural markets to unlock new growth opportunities.

E-commerce has become a game-changer, leveraging India's digital revolution to make shopping seamless, accessible, and inclusive for consumers across urban and rural regions.

These sectors, powered by the middle class, are creating a thriving consumer ecosystem that is setting benchmarks for growth, innovation, and inclusivity.

India: A Thriving Ecosystem of Demand and Innovation

For global brands and entrepreneurs, India is not just a lucrative market—it is a **living laboratory for innovation**, where businesses can test, refine, and scale their products and services to meet diverse consumer needs.

Diverse Opportunities: India's consumer market offers avenues for both luxury and mass-market segments, ensuring that businesses across the price spectrum can find a foothold.

Local Adaptation and Global Insights: Companies entering India often tailor their offerings to local preferences, and in doing so, gain insights that are applicable to other emerging markets worldwide.

Collaborative Growth: Partnerships with local players, government support, and the availability of skilled talent create an environment where businesses can flourish sustainably.

India's middle class is not just consuming—it is co-creating, influencing global trends, and shaping the strategies of some of the world's most recognized brands.

The Road Ahead: A Cornerstone of India's Economic Story

As India's middle class continues to grow—projected to reach **700 million by 2030**—its influence will expand further, driving innovation, investments, and economic growth. This demographic shift is not only reshaping domestic consumption patterns but also positioning India as a key player in the global economy.

For Businesses: India offers an unparalleled opportunity to tap into a diverse, expanding, and increasingly sophisticated consumer base.

For Investors: The country's robust consumer ecosystem, combined with supportive policies and competitive advantages, ensures a high potential for long-term returns.

For Entrepreneurs: India's thriving startup culture, coupled with the middle class's readiness to adopt new ideas, creates an ideal environment for innovation and growth.

Final Thoughts

India's consumer magnetism, driven by its vibrant middle class, is more than a statistic—it is a narrative of aspirations, growth, and transformation. As this demographic continues to expand in size and influence, it will remain the cornerstone of India's economic story, setting the stage for a future that is both **prosperous** and **dynamic**.

For businesses, investors, and entrepreneurs, engaging with India's middle class is not just an opportunity—it is a necessity for those looking to participate in one of the most exciting consumer markets in the world.

10. Overcoming Challenges: Navigating India's Investment Landscape

"Opportunities are often disguised as challenges, and those who adapt thrive."

India's investment landscape offers immense potential, but like any dynamic and evolving market, it presents a unique set of challenges. Bureaucratic hurdles, regulatory complexities, and cultural nuances can create roadblocks for businesses entering or expanding in this vibrant economy. However, with strategic planning, effective risk mitigation, and a willingness to adapt, these obstacles can transform into opportunities for growth and innovation.

This chapter delves into the common challenges faced by investors, the strategies to navigate them successfully, and inspiring real-world examples that highlight how persistence and adaptability lead to success in India's complex yet rewarding market.

Tackling Bureaucratic Hurdles, Regulatory Complexities, and Cultural Nuances

Entering India's dynamic market requires businesses to navigate a multifaceted landscape defined by its regulatory framework, bureaucratic layers, and rich cultural diversity. Success in India depends on understanding and adapting to these challenges with strategic approaches and local insights.

Bureaucratic Hurdles: Simplifying Complexity

India's bureaucratic system, though improving, can still present challenges, especially for businesses unfamiliar with its intricacies.

Delays in Approvals: Obtaining permits and clearances can be a prolonged process due to the involvement of multiple agencies and administrative layers. For example, infrastructure projects may require approvals from central, state, and local authorities, leading to delays in execution.

Inconsistent Processes: Variations in administrative procedures across states can create confusion, especially for businesses operating in multiple regions. Differences in interpretations of laws and requirements can result in compliance discrepancies.

How to Overcome: **Local Expertise**: Engage with local consultants or partners who understand the regional nuances and can expedite processes by navigating the bureaucracy efficiently.

Technology Leverage: Utilize digital platforms like the **National Single Window System (NSWS)**, which streamlines the process of obtaining approvals, licenses, and clearances across sectors.

Proactive Engagement: Build relationships with regulatory authorities to stay informed and minimize delays caused by procedural gaps.

Regulatory Complexities: Adapting to Change

India's regulatory environment is evolving, particularly in high-growth sectors like e-commerce, data protection, and taxation. While these changes aim to create a transparent and robust business ecosystem, they can pose challenges for companies trying to keep pace.

Sector-Specific Challenges:

E-Commerce: Regulations around foreign direct investment (FDI), marketplace models, and consumer protection require constant monitoring.

Taxation: The Goods and Services Tax (GST) has streamlined taxation but requires businesses to stay updated on frequent rate revisions and compliance rules.

Frequent Policy Changes: Policy reforms aimed at improving governance can require businesses to adapt quickly, which may strain resources or disrupt operations.

How to Overcome:

Legal Partnerships: Partner with compliance experts and legal advisors who can provide updates and actionable insights on policy developments.

Industry Forums: Actively participate in forums and industry associations to stay informed, share concerns, and engage with policymakers for clarity and consistency.

Flexibility in Planning: Develop adaptable strategies that allow businesses to pivot quickly in response to regulatory changes.

Cultural Nuances: Understanding the Market's Pulse

India's diversity is one of its greatest strengths but also one of its most complex challenges. The country's varying cultural norms, consumer behaviors, and business practices require a localized approach to succeed.

Regional Differences: Business practices and etiquette vary significantly across regions. For instance, the approach to negotiations in Delhi may differ from that in Chennai or Kolkata. Consumer preferences are shaped by local traditions, languages, and festivals, influencing purchasing behavior.

Trust and Relationships: In many sectors, building trust and long-term relationships is as critical as operational efficiency. Indian businesses often value personal connections alongside professional engagements.

How to Overcome:

Cultural Sensitivity: Invest time in understanding the cultural norms and values of the regions where your business operates. Adapt marketing strategies to reflect local traditions and festivals, which play a significant role in consumer decision-making.

Localized Workforce Management: Employ a culturally diverse workforce that understands regional nuances and can effectively manage local operations. Train employees to embrace cross-cultural communication, ensuring seamless collaboration across teams.

Tailored Consumer Engagement: Customize products and services to align with regional preferences. For instance, offering localized flavors or packaging designs can significantly enhance consumer appeal.

Real-World Application

Navigating India's complex landscape is not without its challenges, but businesses that adapt strategically have achieved remarkable success.

Example:

Amazon India overcame regulatory hurdles by introducing region-specific innovations such as cash-on-delivery and local language support, enabling it to build trust and expand rapidly in diverse markets.

IKEA adapted to cultural nuances by sourcing locally and tailoring its product offerings to meet Indian household needs, such as compact furniture for smaller living spaces.

These examples highlight how a deep understanding of India's regulatory, bureaucratic, and cultural landscape can transform challenges into opportunities for growth.

In conclusion, Tackling bureaucratic hurdles, regulatory complexities, and cultural nuances is an essential part of navigating India's investment landscape. By leveraging local expertise, adopting flexible strategies, and embracing cultural diversity, businesses can turn potential obstacles into stepping stones for success.

India's market is as diverse as it is dynamic, and companies that invest time and effort into understanding its intricacies are well-positioned to thrive in one of the world's most promising economies.

Strategies for Mitigating Risks in New and Evolving Markets

Entering new or rapidly evolving markets like India presents significant opportunities, but it also requires a robust framework to manage risks effectively. With proactive planning, strategic execution, and the use of advanced tools, businesses can navigate uncertainties and build a resilient foundation for growth. Here's how to mitigate risks while expanding into such markets.

Market Research and Entry Strategy: The Foundation of Success

Thorough market research is crucial to understanding the unique dynamics of India's diverse regions and industries.

Understand Regional Demands: India is not a monolithic market; consumer behavior, income levels, and preferences vary widely across states and regions. For example, while Tier 1 cities may demand premium products, rural areas often prioritize affordability and utility.

Assess Competitive Landscapes: Identify competitors, their market strategies, and areas where your business can differentiate itself. Use this insight to position your brand effectively and identify potential gaps in the market.

Tailored Entry Strategies: Choose an entry strategy that aligns with your risk tolerance and business goals:

Direct Investment: Ideal for companies with extensive resources and long-term plans.

Joint Ventures: Leverage the local expertise and networks of established partners.

Partnerships: Collaborate with distributors or suppliers to ease market entry and reduce operational risks.

A well-researched and strategically chosen entry approach ensures a smoother transition into the market and lays the groundwork for sustainable growth.

Local Partnerships: Navigating Market Complexities

Partnering with local businesses is one of the most effective ways to mitigate risks in an unfamiliar market.

Regulatory Navigation: Local partners bring expertise in navigating India's complex regulatory framework, ensuring faster compliance and reducing administrative hurdles. They can help interpret state-specific policies, taxes, and labor laws that may vary widely across the country.

Consumer Insights: Collaborating with local businesses provides valuable insights into consumer preferences, enabling companies to tailor products and marketing strategies accordingly. For example, Coca-Cola's partnership with Indian bottlers allowed it to adapt its distribution and marketing to suit regional needs.

Network Building: Local partnerships facilitate access to established networks, including suppliers, distributors, and customers, accelerating market penetration.

Diversification: Reducing Risk Exposure

Relying too heavily on a single region, product, or sector increases vulnerability to localized risks such as policy changes or economic fluctuations.

Geographical Diversification: Spread investments across multiple states to minimize the impact of regional economic slowdowns, political instability, or policy shifts. For example, setting up operations in both industrialized regions like Maharashtra and emerging markets like Uttar Pradesh can balance risk and growth potential.

Sectoral Diversification: Expand into complementary sectors to reduce dependence on one industry. For instance, a company focusing on FMCG might also explore opportunities in logistics to support supply chain operations.

Adaptable Product Offerings: Tailor product lines to cater to diverse consumer bases across urban and rural markets, ensuring a wider reach and risk spread.

Risk Management: Preparing for the Unexpected

A proactive approach to risk management helps businesses mitigate potential disruptions and safeguard their operations.

Contingency Planning: Develop contingency plans to address challenges such as supply chain disruptions, regulatory changes, or currency fluctuations. For example, establishing multiple supplier relationships can prevent bottlenecks during logistical issues.

Insurance Products: Utilize insurance products to safeguard against unforeseen risks:

Political Risk Insurance: Protects investments from losses due to political instability, expropriation, or currency restrictions.

Supply Chain Insurance: Covers losses from disruptions in production or delivery.

Crisis Response Teams: Establish internal teams dedicated to monitoring risks and responding swiftly to emerging challenges.

Leveraging Technology: Enhancing Operational Resilience

Technology plays a vital role in reducing risks and improving operational efficiency in evolving markets like India.

Streamlined Operations: Use Enterprise Resource Planning (ERP) systems to integrate and manage business processes, ensuring better control and visibility. Automate routine tasks to reduce errors and enhance productivity.

Data-Driven Decision-Making: Leverage AI-driven analytics to gain real-time insights into market trends, customer behavior, and operational efficiency. For instance, predictive analytics can help forecast demand fluctuations, enabling better inventory management.

Digital Compliance Tools: Use digital platforms to monitor regulatory requirements and ensure compliance, reducing the risk of fines or legal complications.

Enhanced Customer Engagement: Employ customer relationship management (CRM) tools to build stronger connections with consumers, tailoring offerings based on preferences and feedback.

Technology not only mitigates risks but also creates a competitive edge by enabling faster, smarter, and more agile operations.

Real-World Application of Strategies

Global companies entering India have successfully navigated risks by implementing these strategies:

Walmart: Partnered with Flipkart to understand the local e-commerce market, leveraging Flipkart's network and expertise to establish its presence.

Hyundai: Diversified its product offerings by introducing models tailored for both urban and rural markets, mitigating risks associated with a single consumer segment.

Nestlé India: Employed predictive analytics to manage its supply chain more effectively, ensuring uninterrupted operations during regulatory changes and disruptions.

In conclusion, mitigating risks in new and evolving markets like India requires a proactive, multi-pronged approach that includes thorough research, strategic partnerships, diversification, robust risk management, and technology adoption.

By employing these strategies, businesses can navigate uncertainties, capitalize on opportunities, and build a resilient foundation for long-term success. In a market as dynamic as India, risk is an inherent part of the journey—but with the right strategies, it can also be a catalyst for innovation and growth.

Real-World Examples of How Investors Overcame Challenges

Success in India's investment landscape often hinges on understanding the market's complexities, embracing innovation, and localizing strategies. The following examples demonstrate how major companies navigated challenges to establish themselves in India and achieve long-term success.

Amazon in India: Redefining E-Commerce

Challenge: Amazon faced India's complex e-commerce regulations, which include restrictions on FDI in inventory-based models, and stiff competition from local players like Flipkart.

Navigating diverse consumer behaviors across urban and rural markets added to the complexity.

Solution:

Localization: Amazon introduced features tailored to Indian consumers, such as **regional language support** and **cash-on-delivery (COD)**, a critical payment method for customers unfamiliar with digital payments.

Partnerships with Local Sellers: By onboarding local businesses and artisans, Amazon expanded its product portfolio and gained consumer trust. Initiatives like **Amazon Saheli** (empowering women entrepreneurs) strengthened community connections.

Supply Chain Investment: Amazon built an extensive logistics network, including warehouses and last-mile delivery systems, to cater to the diverse geographies of India.

Amazon's ability to adapt and localize its strategy has made it a dominant player in India's competitive e-commerce market.

IKEA's Entry: Tailoring the Retail Experience

Challenge: IKEA encountered challenges in navigating India's regulatory environment, particularly the **Foreign Direct Investment (FDI)** rules in retail.

Understanding local consumer behavior was essential, given the preference for affordable, space-efficient furniture and the cultural significance of home decor.

Solution:

Adapting Store Formats: IKEA shifted from its traditional large-format stores to smaller, urban outlets to cater to densely populated cities like Mumbai and Bengaluru.

Local Sourcing: Collaborating with Indian vendors allowed IKEA to meet FDI sourcing requirements while offering locally relevant products.

Tailored Products: IKEA introduced compact furniture and cookware designed for Indian households, aligning with cultural and spatial needs.

IKEA's focus on localization and adaptability has enabled it to establish a strong foothold in India's growing retail sector.

Hyundai in the Automotive Market: Winning Indian Roads

Challenge: Entering a market dominated by Maruti Suzuki required Hyundai to differentiate itself and adapt to Indian preferences for compact, affordable, and fuel-efficient cars.

Solution:

R&D Investment: Hyundai developed models like the **Santro** and **Creta**, specifically designed for Indian consumers. These cars combined affordability with innovative features like enhanced fuel efficiency and compact designs.

Strong Dealership Network: Hyundai established an extensive network of dealerships and service centers to enhance accessibility and build customer trust.

Competitive Pricing: Hyundai positioned its vehicles at price points that balanced affordability with premium features, appealing to both middle-class and aspirational consumers.

Hyundai's India-specific approach has helped it become one of the leading automotive brands in the country.

Unilever (Hindustan Unilever Limited - HUL): Expanding Rural Reach

Challenge: Reaching rural India posed challenges due to inadequate infrastructure, fragmented markets, and price sensitivity among consumers.

Solution:

Rural Distribution Model: HUL developed innovative distribution systems tailored for rural markets, including smaller SKUs (stock-keeping units) that allowed consumers to purchase products in affordable quantities.

Shakti Program: This initiative empowered rural women to become sales agents, expanding HUL's distribution network while promoting economic inclusion.

Localized Marketing: HUL's campaigns highlighted the functional benefits of products like Lifebuoy soap and Wheel detergent, resonating with rural consumers' needs.

HUL's ability to innovate and adapt to rural markets has solidified its status as a market leader in India's FMCG sector.

Lessons Learned: Adaptability, Localization, and Collaboration

These examples highlight key strategies that have enabled companies to overcome challenges in India's complex market:

Adaptability: Successful businesses tailored their operations, products, and services to meet India's diverse consumer preferences.

Localization: From sourcing materials locally to designing India-specific products, localization was critical to gaining consumer trust and loyalty.

Collaboration: Partnering with local businesses, suppliers, and communities allowed companies to navigate regulatory hurdles and establish a deeper connection with their target markets.

In summary, the experiences of Amazon, IKEA, Hyundai, and Unilever demonstrate that while India's investment landscape presents challenges, it also offers unparalleled opportunities for those willing to innovate and adapt. These companies' success stories underscore the importance of cultural sensitivity, market-specific strategies, and robust local partnerships in achieving sustainable growth in one of the world's most dynamic markets.

For businesses eyeing India, these real-world examples serve as a roadmap for overcoming obstacles and unlocking the immense potential of this vibrant economy.

Conclusion

Navigating India's investment landscape is a journey that demands a harmonious blend of **strategic foresight**, **cultural sensitivity**, and **operational resilience**. The country's vast market potential is matched by its complexities—bureaucratic hurdles, regulatory intricacies, and diverse cultural nuances that can pose significant challenges to unwary investors. However, these obstacles are not insurmountable. With the right approach, they can be transformed into stepping stones toward success.

Turning Challenges into Opportunities

Strategic Foresight: Investors must engage in meticulous planning, understanding not just the current market dynamics but also anticipating future trends. This involves staying abreast of policy changes, economic indicators, and technological advancements that could impact their ventures. Strategic foresight enables businesses to position themselves advantageously, capitalizing on emerging opportunities while mitigating risks.

Cultural Sensitivity: India's rich tapestry of languages, traditions, and social norms means that a one-size-fits-all strategy is unlikely to succeed. Cultural sensitivity goes beyond mere acknowledgment of differences; it requires a deep engagement with local customs, consumer behaviors, and business etiquettes. By embracing cultural nuances, companies can build strong relationships with stakeholders, earn customer loyalty, and enhance their brand reputation.

Operational Resilience: The ability to adapt to changing circumstances is crucial in India's dynamic environment. Operational resilience involves developing robust systems that can withstand regulatory shifts, market volatility, and logistical challenges. It also means being agile enough to pivot strategies in response to unforeseen events, ensuring continuity and sustainability.

Leveraging Strategies for Success

By learning from real-world examples, investors can adopt proven strategies to navigate India's market effectively:

Local Partnerships: Collaborating with local businesses, as seen with companies like Amazon and IKEA, provides invaluable insights into the regulatory landscape and consumer preferences. These partnerships can facilitate smoother market entry, enhance distribution networks, and foster innovation through the exchange of ideas.

Risk Diversification: Spreading investments across different regions and sectors reduces exposure to localized risks. Companies like Hyundai diversified their product offerings to cater to various market segments, thereby minimizing the impact of regional economic fluctuations or policy changes.

Technology Adoption: Embracing digital tools and advanced technologies can streamline operations, improve compliance, and offer competitive advantages. Businesses that leverage technology, such as Unilever with its data-driven supply chain management, can enhance efficiency and responsiveness to market demands.

Adaptability and Innovation: Success in India often hinges on a company's ability to adapt its products and services to meet local needs. By investing in research and development, companies can innovate solutions that resonate with Indian consumers, driving growth and establishing market leadership.

India: A Land of Immense Opportunity

India's investment landscape is as challenging as it is rewarding. The nation's economy is one of the fastest-growing in the world, characterized by a young population, a burgeoning middle class, and a government committed to reform and development. These factors contribute to an environment ripe with opportunities for those willing to navigate its complexities.

Economic Growth: India's GDP growth presents vast opportunities across sectors such as technology, infrastructure, healthcare, and consumer goods. Investors can tap into markets that are expanding both in scale and sophistication.

Innovation Hub: With a thriving startup ecosystem and a focus on digital transformation, India is emerging as a global innovation hub. This environment encourages experimentation and rewards disruptive ideas, providing fertile ground for entrepreneurial ventures.

Strategic Positioning: India's geographic location and international relationships position it as a gateway to other emerging markets in Asia and beyond. Investments in India can serve as a strategic foothold for broader regional expansion.

The Path Forward

For investors and businesses, the journey in India is not just about overcoming obstacles—it is about leveraging them to create **innovative solutions** and build a **lasting impact** in one of the world's most dynamic markets. Success requires patience, persistence, and a proactive approach to understanding and integrating into the local context.

Building Relationships: Long-term success in India is often built on strong relationships with customers, partners, and government entities. Trust and credibility are essential assets that can be cultivated through transparency, ethical practices, and social responsibility.

Continuous Learning: The Indian market is ever-evolving, necessitating a commitment to continuous learning and adaptation. Staying informed about regulatory changes, consumer trends, and technological advancements is critical for maintaining a competitive edge.

Commitment to Excellence: Delivering high-quality products and services that meet the needs and expectations of Indian consumers is fundamental. Companies that prioritize excellence and customer satisfaction are more likely to achieve sustainable growth.

Embracing the Opportunity

As India continues to grow and evolve, it remains a land of immense opportunity. The challenges that come with its vast and varied landscape are matched by the potential for significant rewards. Investors who can **adapt**, **innovate**, and **persevere** will find that India offers not just a market, but a partner in growth and a platform for global impact.

In embracing the complexities of India's investment landscape, businesses are not only expanding their horizons but also contributing to the country's development journey. Together, they are shaping a future marked by shared prosperity, innovation, and resilience.

11. Real Stories: India's Investment Success Stories

India's vibrant and evolving market has been a fertile ground for remarkable success stories, where both domestic and global investors have not only navigated challenges but also capitalized on the country's immense opportunities. By embracing India's unique dynamics, adapting strategies to local needs, and fostering collaborations, these businesses have carved a path to long-term growth and success.

This chapter explores inspiring case studies of companies thriving in India, the invaluable lessons their journeys offer, and the collaborative ventures that highlight India's potential as a premier investment destination.

Case Studies of Companies Thriving in India

Tata Starbucks: Localizing a Global Brand

Tata Starbucks stands as a testament to how global brands can succeed in India by embracing localization and cultural sensitivity. A joint venture between Tata Global Beverages and Starbucks, this partnership exemplifies the seamless blending of international expertise with local insights, creating a brand that resonates deeply with Indian consumers.

Understanding Local Preferences: The Foundation of Success

When Starbucks entered India, it recognized that replicating its global model without adaptation wouldn't suffice in a culturally diverse and cost-sensitive market. To cater to Indian tastes, Tata Starbucks introduced a menu that combined global favorites with local flavors. Items like **masala chai** and **tandoori paneer sandwiches** were designed to appeal to Indian palates, offering familiarity alongside the signature Starbucks experience.

The incorporation of these India-specific offerings wasn't just about menu innovation—it was a strategic move to connect with consumers who value their cultural identity even as they explore global brands.

Premium Positioning: Building Aspirational Value

In a market where coffee consumption was historically overshadowed by tea, Tata Starbucks positioned itself not just as a coffee brand but as a **lifestyle choice**. Its stores became urban havens for the middle-class and affluent consumers, offering a blend of luxury, comfort, and community.

The brand's emphasis on quality, ambiance, and personalized service struck a chord with India's growing urban demographic, for whom Starbucks represented both indulgence and aspiration. This premium positioning helped Starbucks carve a niche in a competitive market filled with local coffee houses and tea stalls.

Strategic Locations: Capturing Urban Footfall

Location played a pivotal role in Tata Starbucks' expansion strategy. The brand carefully selected **high-traffic urban areas** such as malls, airports, and tech parks for its outlets, ensuring visibility and accessibility to its target audience. These locations also catered to the growing segment of young professionals and students who frequented these spaces for both leisure and work.

In addition to Tier 1 cities like Mumbai, Delhi, and Bengaluru, Tata Starbucks began expanding into **Tier 2 cities**, tapping into the aspirations of a burgeoning middle class. Cities like Pune, Chandigarh, and Lucknow became key growth hubs, reflecting Starbucks' commitment to reaching beyond metropolitan India.

Impact: A Prominent Name in India's Coffee Segment

Tata Starbucks' localized approach has paid off handsomely, transforming the brand into a leading name in India's premium coffee segment. Its ability to adapt to local tastes while maintaining the essence of the global Starbucks experience has made it a preferred choice among urban consumers.

Today, Tata Starbucks operates hundreds of stores across India, with ambitious plans for further expansion. The brand's journey underscores the importance of cultural adaptation, strategic positioning, and collaboration with local partners in thriving within India's diverse and competitive market.

Tata Starbucks' success is a blueprint for global brands looking to enter India—it's not just about bringing a product to the market but about **understanding and engaging with the soul of the market itself**. By striking the right balance between localization and premium global appeal, Tata Starbucks has created a model of enduring success.

Reliance Jio: Transforming Digital Connectivity

Reliance Jio's entry into India's telecom market marked a watershed moment, fundamentally altering the country's digital landscape. A disruptive force spearheaded by Reliance Industries, Jio reshaped consumer behavior, democratized internet access, and set the stage for India's digital revolution. Its success story is a masterclass in innovation, strategic investment, and market disruption.

Revolutionizing Access with Disruptive Pricing

Before Jio's launch in 2016, internet access in India was expensive and largely limited to urban areas. Reliance Jio turned this narrative on its head with an aggressive pricing strategy that offered **free voice calls** and **ultra-low-cost data packages**, making connectivity accessible to millions.

This disruptive approach wasn't just about affordability—it was about inclusivity. By removing cost barriers, Jio empowered people across all income groups to access high-speed internet, fundamentally changing how Indians consumed content, communicated, and conducted business.

The pricing strategy quickly helped Jio amass millions of subscribers, creating one of the largest customer bases in the telecom industry in record time. By prioritizing scale and accessibility, Reliance Jio turned connectivity into a necessity rather than a luxury.

Building a Digital Ecosystem: Beyond Connectivity

Reliance Jio didn't stop at providing affordable telecom services. It envisioned a **digital ecosystem** that would enhance the value of its network and keep users engaged.

Entertainment Platforms: Jio launched a suite of apps, including **JioTV**, **JioCinema**, and **JioSaavn**, offering on-demand entertainment, music streaming, and live television. These services transformed Jio into a lifestyle brand that catered to India's burgeoning appetite for digital content.

Productivity Tools: The ecosystem extended to tools like **JioMeet** (video conferencing) and **JioChat** (instant messaging), ensuring relevance in both personal and professional spheres.

E-Commerce and Payments: Jio also ventured into digital commerce and payments, enabling users to shop and transact seamlessly within its ecosystem.

This comprehensive approach turned Jio from a telecom provider into an integral part of India's digital journey, creating unparalleled customer loyalty and engagement.

Infrastructure Investment: Bridging the Urban-Rural Divide

One of Jio's most remarkable achievements was its investment in infrastructure, enabling seamless connectivity across the length and breadth of the country. Reliance Jio built a state-of-the-art **4G network**, ensuring high-speed internet even in remote areas that had previously been underserved or entirely unconnected.

Urban Reach: In cities, Jio's robust infrastructure provided reliable and fast connectivity, catering to the needs of tech-savvy urban consumers and businesses.

Rural Penetration: In rural areas, Jio's affordable services and extensive coverage empowered communities, giving them access to information, education, and economic opportunities.

Reliance Jio's infrastructure investment was not just about technology—it was about inclusion, bridging the digital divide, and bringing the benefits of connectivity to every corner of India.

Impact: Accelerating India's Digital Transformation

The impact of Reliance Jio on India's digital ecosystem has been nothing short of revolutionary:

Digital Adoption: Jio's entry catalyzed a rapid increase in internet usage, making the internet an integral part of everyday life. From streaming and online shopping to remote work and education, Jio redefined how India interacted with technology.

Market Disruption: Jio's pricing strategy forced competitors to lower their rates, making digital connectivity more affordable across the board.

Economic Growth: By enabling millions of people and businesses to go online, Jio contributed to economic growth, fostering innovation, entrepreneurship, and job creation. Reliance Jio's transformation of the telecom industry has positioned India as one of the largest and fastest-growing digital markets in the world.

In summary, Reliance Jio's story is a remarkable example of how bold vision, strategic execution, and customer-centric innovation can redefine an industry. By democratizing internet access and building a holistic digital ecosystem, Jio has not only transformed connectivity but has also empowered millions to participate in India's digital economy.

For investors and businesses, Jio's journey underscores the immense potential of combining disruptive strategies with long-term investment, making it a cornerstone of India's digital transformation narrative.

Hyundai Motors: Winning Indian Roads

Hyundai Motors' journey in India is a testament to the power of localization, innovation, and strategic planning. Entering a market dominated by Maruti Suzuki, Hyundai faced the challenge of establishing itself in a competitive landscape. Yet, with a focus on understanding Indian consumers and addressing their specific needs, Hyundai not only gained a foothold but quickly rose to become one of India's leading automotive brands.

Breaking Into a Competitive Market

When Hyundai entered India in the late 1990s, Maruti Suzuki held an overwhelming market share, with its affordable and reliable cars setting the benchmark for Indian consumers. Hyundai recognized that succeeding in this environment required more than offering global models—it required tailoring products and strategies to meet the unique demands of Indian buyers.

Key Strategies Driving Hyundai's Success

India-Specific R&D: Building Cars for Indian Roads

Hyundai invested heavily in **research and development (R&D)** to design vehicles that suited India's diverse terrains, climate conditions, and consumer preferences.

Its first offering, the **Hyundai Santro**, was a compact, fuel-efficient car that immediately resonated with Indian families seeking affordability, reliability, and modern features.

Over the years, Hyundai continued to develop models like the **Creta**, a compact SUV that captured the aspirations of urban consumers looking for style, space, and performance.

By addressing the evolving needs of Indian consumers, Hyundai positioned itself as a brand that understood and catered to local preferences.

Extensive Network: Bringing the Brand Closer to Consumers

Hyundai established a robust **dealership and service network** across the country, ensuring accessibility for customers in both urban and rural areas.

Its focus on after-sales service, combined with affordable maintenance costs, helped build trust and loyalty among Indian buyers.

The widespread network not only boosted sales but also enhanced Hyundai's reputation as a reliable and customer-centric brand.

Localization: Enhancing Affordability and Efficiency

Hyundai achieved an impressive **90% localization** in manufacturing, sourcing components and materials domestically to reduce production costs and improve efficiency.

This strategy enabled the company to price its cars competitively while maintaining high quality.

Localization also allowed Hyundai to adapt quickly to changes in market demand, ensuring a steady supply of vehicles tailored to Indian preferences.

Impact: Driving to the Top

Hyundai's approach paid off, and its impact on the Indian automotive market has been profound:

Market Leadership: Hyundai is now the **second-largest car manufacturer in India**, with a diverse portfolio of vehicles catering to various customer segments. Models like the Santro, i20, Creta, and Venue have become household names, cementing Hyundai's position as a trusted and aspirational brand.

Loyal Customer Base: Hyundai's commitment to quality, affordability, and customer satisfaction has earned it a loyal following, with many buyers returning for upgrades within the Hyundai family.

Innovation and Growth: Hyundai's continued investment in R&D and innovation, including the introduction of electric vehicles (EVs) like the Kona Electric, reflects its adaptability to market trends and its vision for sustainable mobility.

In short, Hyundai Motors' success in India is a story of adaptation, perseverance, and consumer focus. By investing in India-specific R&D, building an extensive network, and embracing localization, Hyundai transformed itself into a leading player in one of the world's most competitive automotive markets.

For global businesses looking to succeed in India, Hyundai's journey offers valuable lessons: understand the market deeply, cater to local needs, and build trust through quality and accessibility. Today, Hyundai's cars are not just vehicles on Indian roads—they are symbols of innovation, reliability, and aspiration, reflecting the company's deep connection with the Indian consumer.

Lessons Learned from Successful Ventures

The success stories of Tata Starbucks, Reliance Jio, and Hyundai Motors underscore the immense potential of India's market, but they also highlight the critical strategies required to thrive in its dynamic and complex environment. Each of these companies, through their unique journeys, has provided valuable insights into what it takes to succeed in India—a market defined by its diversity, growth opportunities, and challenges.

Adaptability Is Key

India's diversity, both cultural and economic, demands a high level of adaptability from businesses.

Why It Matters: With its 1.4 billion people, India is not one homogenous market but a collection of distinct regions, each with its own language, customs, and consumer preferences. A product that works in urban Bengaluru may not resonate with rural Uttar Pradesh.

Lessons from Tata Starbucks: Starbucks' success lies in its ability to **tailor its offerings** to Indian tastes, introducing items like masala chai and tandoori paneer sandwiches. By blending global standards with local flavors, the brand ensured its appeal to a wide demographic.

Key Takeaway: Businesses must be flexible in their approach, whether by customizing products, rethinking marketing strategies, or adjusting operations to align with local needs. Adaptability ensures relevance and acceptance in a diverse market like India.

Local Partnerships Matter

Navigating India's regulatory landscape and understanding its market dynamics can be daunting for new entrants. Local partnerships can bridge these gaps.

Why It Matters: Collaborating with established local players provides invaluable **insights, networks, and resources.** It also helps businesses navigate regulatory requirements and cultural nuances more effectively.

Lessons from Reliance Jio: Jio's ecosystem benefited from partnerships with local app developers and content creators, which enriched its offerings and built a strong connect with Indian consumers. Similarly, Starbucks partnered with the Tata Group, leveraging Tata's local expertise and credibility to establish itself in India.

Key Takeaway: Partnering with local stakeholders not only reduces operational risks but also accelerates market penetration by providing a foundation of trust and familiarity.

Price Sensitivity Is Crucial

India's consumer base is diverse in its spending power, with a significant portion of the population being highly price-sensitive. Understanding and catering to this sensitivity is vital.

Why It Matters: While there is a growing demand for premium products, affordability remains a key factor for a large segment of the market. Balancing quality and cost is critical for widespread adoption.

Lessons from Hyundai Motors: Hyundai's success in India was built on its ability to offer **affordable, fuel-efficient cars** like the Santro, which catered to the needs of middle-class families. It struck the perfect balance between price and quality, making its vehicles accessible while maintaining brand value.

Key Takeaway: Businesses should design pricing strategies that reflect the purchasing power of their target audience. Offering smaller, affordable variants or tiered pricing can open up multiple consumer segments.

Infrastructure Investment Drives Growth

Building the necessary infrastructure—whether physical, digital, or logistical—is often a prerequisite for long-term success in India.

Why It Matters: A lack of robust infrastructure in certain areas can hinder business growth. Companies that invest in their own infrastructure can not only overcome these challenges but also gain a competitive edge.

Lessons from Reliance Jio: Jio invested heavily in creating a **pan-India 4G network**, ensuring high-speed internet access even in rural and underserved areas. This investment laid the foundation for its massive success, enabling it to deliver on its promise of affordable connectivity.

Key Takeaway: Long-term success in India often requires significant **upfront investment in infrastructure**. Whether it's setting up manufacturing units, supply chains, or digital networks, these investments ensure scalability and resilience.

Brand Trust Is Essential

Indian consumers place a high value on **trust and transparency**, often choosing brands that demonstrate reliability and integrity.

Why It Matters: Building trust is not just about delivering quality products—it's also about being transparent, ethical, and customer-centric in your approach.

Lessons from Tata Starbucks and Hyundai: Starbucks earned trust through consistent quality and customer service, while Hyundai's extensive service network and reliable vehicles made it a household name. Both companies demonstrated a long-term commitment to their customers, fostering loyalty.

Key Takeaway: Businesses must focus on building trust through **quality, transparency, and ethical practices**. A trusted brand is more likely to gain repeat customers and navigate challenges like competition or economic downturns effectively.

In conclusion, the success of Tata Starbucks, Reliance Jio, and Hyundai Motors in India provides a roadmap for businesses looking to enter or expand in the country. **Adaptability**, **local partnerships**, **price sensitivity**, **infrastructure investment**, and **brand trust** are not just strategies—they are imperatives for navigating the complexities of India's market.

India's vast and diverse landscape offers unparalleled opportunities, but capturing them requires a deep understanding of its nuances and a commitment to long-term growth. These lessons underscore the importance of not just entering the market, but thriving within it by addressing its unique challenges and leveraging its immense potential. For investors and entrepreneurs, India remains a land where innovative strategies and thoughtful execution can lead to enduring success.

Stories of Collaboration between Local and Global Investors

Collaboration between local and global players has been a cornerstone of success for many businesses in India. By combining global expertise with local insights, these partnerships have not only overcome challenges but also redefined industries. Here are three inspiring examples of how such collaborations have shaped India's economic landscape.

Walmart and Flipkart: E-Commerce Powerhouse

Walmart's acquisition of Flipkart for $16 billion in 2018 marked a significant milestone in India's business history, representing one of the largest foreign investments in the country. This partnership blended Walmart's global retail expertise with Flipkart's intimate understanding of the Indian e-commerce landscape.

Strategies for Success

Leveraging Local Expertise: Flipkart's deep knowledge of Indian e-commerce, particularly in navigating regional preferences and regulatory requirements, enabled Walmart to adapt its operations seamlessly. Flipkart's strengths in areas like **cash-on-delivery (COD)** and regional language support were pivotal in building consumer trust and driving adoption.

Supply Chain Innovation: Walmart brought its **logistics and supply chain expertise**, enhancing Flipkart's delivery efficiency. Investments in warehousing, inventory management, and last-mile delivery networks strengthened Flipkart's ability to serve customers across diverse geographies.

Consumer-Centric Approach: Flipkart's understanding of Indian consumer behavior, including preferences for affordable products and flexible payment options, allowed Walmart to tailor its offerings. Initiatives like **Big Billion Days**, Flipkart's flagship sales event, resonated with Indian shoppers and reinforced Flipkart's leadership in the market.

Impact

This collaboration has solidified Flipkart's position as a leader in India's e-commerce space. By blending local expertise with Walmart's global strengths, the partnership has successfully addressed India's unique challenges, such as fragmented logistics and price-sensitive consumers. Walmart's entry into the Indian digital economy through Flipkart underscores the importance of localization and strategic alliances in penetrating complex markets.

Maruti Suzuki: A Model of Indo-Japanese Synergy

The joint venture between Maruti Udyog and Suzuki Motor Corporation, established in 1982, is a shining example of how international and domestic partnerships can transform industries. Together, they created a market leader in India's automotive sector, redefining mobility for millions.

Strategies for Success

Affordable Mobility: Maruti Suzuki focused on delivering cars that met the needs of India's growing middle class. By emphasizing **affordability, fuel efficiency, and durability**, models like the Maruti 800 became iconic symbols of accessible transportation.

Manufacturing Excellence: Leveraging Suzuki's expertise in automotive manufacturing, the partnership established a **robust production ecosystem**. This included state-of-the-art facilities, lean manufacturing practices, and quality assurance systems tailored to Indian conditions.

Dealer Network Expansion: Maruti Suzuki built one of the **largest dealership and service networks** in India, ensuring customers had easy access to sales, maintenance, and support. This extensive network became a critical driver of customer satisfaction and loyalty.

Impact

With a market share of over 40%, Maruti Suzuki dominates India's automotive market. Its enduring success highlights the importance of affordability, localization, and a strong support ecosystem. The partnership has not only created economic value but also revolutionized personal mobility in India.

IKEA and Local Partnerships: Bringing Global Home Furnishings to India

IKEA's entry into India involved strategic collaborations with local vendors, suppliers, and artisans, ensuring the global furniture giant could navigate regulatory requirements and resonate with Indian consumers.

Strategies for Success

Local Sourcing: IKEA partnered with Indian businesses to source over **30% of its materials locally**, complying with **Foreign Direct Investment (FDI)** regulations and reducing costs. This approach also fostered job creation and strengthened local supply chains.

Regional Adaptation: Understanding the space constraints and cultural preferences of Indian households, IKEA adapted its product range and store formats. For instance, compact furniture and cookware designed for Indian kitchens became part of its offering, ensuring greater relevance and appeal.

Skill Development: IKEA invested in **training local artisans and workers**, ensuring that its products met global quality standards while promoting sustainability. Initiatives to empower small-scale industries and craft communities further reinforced IKEA's commitment to India.

Impact

IKEA has successfully established itself as a trusted brand in India, expanding into urban and semi-urban markets. Its ability to localize products, store formats, and sourcing practices has positioned it as a leader in the home furnishings space, catering to the aspirations of India's growing middle class.

Key Takeaways from Collaborative Success Stories

These stories underscore the importance of collaboration in achieving success in India's complex market:

Local Expertise Matters: Global players like Walmart, Suzuki, and IKEA relied on local partners to navigate India's regulatory landscape, consumer behavior, and distribution challenges.

Customization Is Key: Tailoring products and services to local preferences ensures greater acceptance and customer loyalty.

Investing in Infrastructure: Robust supply chains, localized sourcing, and extensive dealership networks enhance operational efficiency and consumer trust.

Long-Term Vision: These partnerships were built with a commitment to long-term growth, focusing on sustainable practices and community engagement.

The stories of Walmart and Flipkart, Maruti Suzuki, and IKEA illustrate how collaboration between local and global investors can unlock immense potential in India. By leveraging each other's strengths, these partnerships have not only overcome challenges but also created value for businesses and consumers alike.

For investors eyeing India, these examples highlight the transformative power of combining global expertise with local insights—a formula that continues to drive success in one of the world's most promising markets.

Conclusion

The success stories of Tata Starbucks, Reliance Jio, Hyundai Motors, Walmart and Flipkart, Maruti Suzuki, and IKEA vividly illustrate the immense potential of India's investment landscape. These examples underscore that while India's market comes with its own complexities, businesses that prioritize **localization**, **collaboration**, and **strategic innovation** can not only navigate these challenges but also thrive.

Localization: Understanding the Indian Consumer

The key to success in India lies in embracing its diversity. With its unique cultural, linguistic, and economic nuances, India demands that businesses go beyond their global models and adapt to local needs.

Companies like **Tata Starbucks** have demonstrated that tailoring products to local tastes—such as introducing masala chai and tandoori paneer sandwiches—can create deep connections with consumers.

Similarly, **IKEA's approach** of designing compact furniture and cookware to suit Indian households showcases the power of catering to local lifestyles.

Localization isn't just about products; it extends to pricing, marketing, and customer engagement, ensuring businesses resonate with the aspirations and preferences of Indian consumers.

Collaboration: Building on Local Strengths

Collaborating with local partners has proven to be a winning strategy for global investors. Partnerships provide insights into India's regulatory landscape, market dynamics, and consumer behavior.

Flipkart's partnership with Walmart combined the former's local expertise with the latter's global resources, creating a formidable e-commerce powerhouse.

Maruti Suzuki's enduring joint venture is another prime example of how global expertise in manufacturing, combined with local market knowledge, can transform industries and drive sustained success.

Collaboration not only facilitates market entry but also builds trust and fosters innovation, enabling businesses to navigate India's complexities with confidence.

Strategic Innovation: Adapting and Leading

India's dynamic market rewards companies that innovate strategically and invest in long-term growth.

Reliance Jio's digital ecosystem exemplifies how businesses can go beyond core offerings to create value-added services that enhance customer loyalty.

Hyundai Motors' investment in R&D to design India-specific cars like the Santro and Creta reflects the importance of innovation tailored to market needs.

Innovation also extends to business models, as seen in **HUL's rural distribution network**, which leveraged smaller SKUs and empowered rural women to expand its reach. Strategic innovation ensures that businesses remain agile, competitive, and relevant in India's rapidly evolving market.

A Blueprint for Success

For investors, these success stories provide a blueprint for navigating India's challenges and unlocking its immense opportunities. Key takeaways include:

Adaptability: Be flexible in operations, products, and strategies to meet India's diverse consumer needs.

Long-Term Vision: Focus on sustainable growth by investing in infrastructure, innovation, and community engagement.

Consumer-Centric Approach: Build trust and loyalty by understanding and addressing consumer aspirations and challenges.

India's market is not a sprint but a marathon—success comes to those who commit to understanding its intricacies and fostering lasting relationships.

India's Role in the Global Economy

As one of the fastest-growing major economies, India plays a pivotal role in shaping global business trends. Its young population, burgeoning middle class, and government focus on reform and development create an environment ripe with opportunities. For businesses willing to embrace the market's complexity, India offers a platform for innovation, growth, and global influence.

The Way Forward

India's investment landscape is as challenging as it is rewarding. By learning from these real-world stories, businesses can position themselves not just as participants but as contributors to India's remarkable economic journey. Success in India is about more than financial gains—it's about being part of a transformative story that impacts lives, empowers communities, and shapes the future.

For those ready to **adapt**, **collaborate**, and **innovate**, India remains a land of immense potential—a dynamic market where challenges turn into opportunities and investments yield both impact and returns.

12. Future Magnetism: What Lies Ahead for India

***"The future belongs to those who prepare for it today."* – Malcolm X**

India stands at the threshold of a transformative era, ready to redefine its role as a global leader. With a relentless focus on innovation, sustainability, and policy-driven growth, the nation is rapidly embracing the industries of the future while setting ambitious long-term goals that align with its aspirations. From pioneering advancements in space technology and artificial intelligence to shaping a fintech revolution, India is positioning itself as a beacon of opportunity for investors and innovators worldwide.

This chapter delves into the emerging trends shaping India's future, its centenary vision for 2047, and the critical role of policy reforms and innovation in unlocking its potential as a global economic powerhouse.

Emerging Trends: Shaping tomorrow's Industries

India's future magnetism lies in its ability to harness cutting-edge technologies and foster industries that drive global progress.

Space Technology: Launching a New Frontier

India's journey in space technology has been nothing short of extraordinary, capturing global attention for its ingenuity, cost-efficiency, and bold ambitions. Led by the **Indian Space Research Organisation (ISRO)**, the nation has consistently pushed the boundaries of exploration, achieving feats that have placed it firmly among the world's leading space-faring nations.

Global Acclaim Through Remarkable Achievements

ISRO's accomplishments are a testament to India's capability to combine technological prowess with cost-effective execution. Missions like

Chandrayaan-3, which successfully landed on the Moon's south pole, and the **Aditya-L1 Solar Mission**, designed to study the Sun, have demonstrated India's expertise in tackling complex challenges in space exploration.

Chandrayaan-3: India became the first country to land on the Moon's south pole, a region critical for understanding lunar resources and potential habitation prospects. This mission not only advanced scientific knowledge but also showcased India's ability to execute such projects at a fraction of the cost of other nations.

Aditya-L1 Solar Mission: A pioneering mission aimed at studying solar activities and their impact on space weather, underscoring India's commitment to contributing to global scientific endeavors.

These achievements underscore India's capability to deliver cutting-edge solutions in space technology while maintaining an unparalleled focus on affordability and efficiency.

Emergence of a Thriving Private Space Ecosystem

Beyond ISRO's accomplishments, India is witnessing the rise of a vibrant **private space sector**, fueled by startups like **Skyroot Aerospace** and **Agnikul Cosmos.**

Skyroot Aerospace: Known for launching India's first privately built rocket, Skyroot is paving the way for **cost-effective satellite launches** and fostering innovation in reusable rocket technology.

Agnikul Cosmos: Specializing in customizable small satellite launches, Agnikul is addressing the growing demand for flexible, on-demand satellite deployment.

These startups, supported by a growing ecosystem of investors and government initiatives, are transforming India's space sector into a dynamic, collaborative arena. Their focus extends beyond satellite launches to areas like **space tourism**, **interplanetary research**, and **commercial space exploration**, positioning India as a competitive player in the global space economy.

Transformative Applications of Space Technology

The impact of India's advancements in space technology goes far beyond exploration. The applications of these technologies are driving transformation across critical sectors:

Communication: Satellites launched by ISRO and private players are bridging connectivity gaps, particularly in remote and underserved regions, enabling better access to digital services and education.

Agriculture: Space-based remote sensing technology is revolutionizing farming by providing data on soil health, weather patterns, and crop conditions, empowering farmers to make informed decisions.

Disaster Management: India's satellite systems play a crucial role in predicting natural disasters, tracking cyclones, and providing early warnings, minimizing loss of life and property.

These practical applications highlight the immense potential of space technology to address real-world challenges, underscoring its value as a driver of economic growth and societal progress.

Positioning India as a Global Leader in Space

India's achievements in space are not just about technological milestones—they reflect a broader ambition to become a leader in the **global space economy**, which is projected to reach $1 trillion by 2040.

Competitive Edge: India's ability to deliver high-quality missions at competitive costs makes it an attractive partner for international collaborations.

Global Partnerships: Through initiatives like the **Gaganyaan Human Spaceflight Program** and collaborative missions with countries like the US, France, and Japan, India is strengthening its role as a key player in global space exploration.

The Road Ahead

As India continues to invest in space technology, its focus on innovation, cost-efficiency, and collaboration ensures that it will remain a significant force in shaping the future of space exploration. The rise of private space startups, coupled with ISRO's ambitious roadmap, positions India not just as a participant but as a leader in the global space economy.

India's space journey exemplifies how strategic investments, collaboration, and visionary leadership can turn challenges into opportunities, propelling a nation to new heights in the pursuit of scientific and technological excellence.

Fintech Revolution: Transforming Financial Ecosystems

India's financial ecosystem is undergoing a radical transformation, driven by the fintech revolution that has reshaped how individuals and businesses access and manage money. From seamless payment solutions to advanced lending platforms, the country's fintech sector is leading the charge in democratizing financial services, making them accessible to millions across urban and rural India.

A Booming Sector Fueled by Innovation

India's fintech sector is now among the fastest-growing globally, projected to reach a market size of $200 billion by 2030. Central to this growth is the **Unified Payments Interface (UPI)**, a game-changing innovation that has revolutionized digital payments.

UPI: The Heartbeat of Digital Transactions

Launched in 2016, UPI has become the backbone of India's payment ecosystem, enabling instantaneous, cost-free money transfers.

With billions of transactions processed monthly, UPI's user-friendly interface and interoperability have made it the preferred mode of payment for individuals and businesses alike.

The introduction of features like **UPI Lite** for offline transactions and **cross-border UPI integration** with countries like Singapore is further cementing its global relevance.

UPI exemplifies how India has harnessed technology to create scalable, inclusive financial solutions that cater to diverse needs, from small vendors to multinational corporations.

Innovations Transforming Financial Services

India's fintech landscape extends beyond payments, with cutting-edge technologies revolutionizing various aspects of financial services:

Digital Lending Platforms: Platforms like **Lendingkart** and **KreditBee** are providing quick, hassle-free loans to small businesses and individuals who previously lacked access to credit. AI-driven credit scoring models analyze alternative data, enabling lenders to assess creditworthiness even for those without formal credit histories.

Robo-Advisors: Automated investment platforms like **Zerodha's Coin** and **Groww** are making wealth management accessible to first-time investors. By using algorithms to offer personalized financial advice, robo-advisors cater to a wide range of investors, from millennials to seasoned professionals.

Blockchain-Based Solutions: Blockchain is being leveraged for secure, transparent transactions, particularly in areas like **trade finance**, **remittances**, and **digital identity verification**. Startups like **Polygon** are positioning India as a hub for blockchain innovation, attracting global partnerships and investments.

These advancements are not just enhancing convenience but are also addressing financial inclusion by bridging gaps in credit, investment, and security.

Policy Frameworks Enabling Growth

The Indian government and regulatory bodies have played a pivotal role in fostering the fintech ecosystem, introducing forward-looking policies and frameworks:

Account Aggregator Framework: This system allows individuals and businesses to share their financial data securely with lenders and financial institutions. By providing a unified view of financial information, it enhances access to credit and empowers consumers to make informed financial decisions.

Regulatory Sandbox Programs: The Reserve Bank of India (RBI) and other regulators have established sandbox environments where fintech companies can test innovative solutions under controlled conditions. This encourages experimentation and reduces the time to market for new financial technologies.

These initiatives not only encourage innovation but also ensure that the fintech sector remains regulated, secure, and aligned with consumer needs.

Driving Financial Inclusion and Empowerment

One of the most transformative aspects of India's fintech revolution is its impact on financial inclusion:

Empowering Underserved Populations: Fintech solutions are bringing banking and credit services to previously unbanked and underserved communities, particularly in rural areas. Initiatives like **Jan Dhan Yojana**, which links bank accounts with digital payment systems, have integrated millions into the formal financial ecosystem.

Boosting MSMEs: Micro, Small, and Medium Enterprises (MSMEs) are benefiting from digital lending and payment platforms, enabling them to scale operations and participate in the digital economy.

Women and Financial Independence: Fintech is empowering women entrepreneurs through access to microloans and digital financial tools, fostering greater participation in economic activities.

Global Leadership in Fintech Innovation

India's fintech journey is not just about solving domestic challenges—it's about setting global benchmarks. The country's leadership in developing scalable solutions like UPI has drawn international attention, with other nations seeking to replicate its success.

Cross-Border Collaborations: Partnerships with countries like Singapore, UAE, and Bhutan for UPI integration are creating new avenues for global fintech expansion.

Startups on the Rise: With over 25 fintech unicorns, India is nurturing a vibrant ecosystem that attracts investments from global players such as Sequoia, SoftBank, and Tiger Global.

In conclusion, India's fintech revolution is a powerful testament to how innovation and policy support can transform an entire sector. By leveraging technologies like UPI, blockchain, and AI, the country is not only enhancing financial accessibility and efficiency but also empowering millions to participate in the digital economy.

As India continues to build on its fintech success, its focus on inclusion, security, and scalability ensures that it remains at the forefront of global financial innovation. For investors and innovators, India's fintech sector represents an unparalleled opportunity to shape the future of finance while contributing to a more inclusive and equitable world.

AI-Driven Industries: The Age of Automation and Intelligence

Artificial Intelligence (AI) is at the forefront of the technological revolution, transforming industries worldwide and unlocking unprecedented opportunities for growth and innovation. In India, AI is not just a tool for modernization—it is a catalyst for solving some of the nation's most pressing challenges while positioning the country as a global hub for AI-driven advancements. From healthcare to agriculture and urban planning, AI is reshaping how industries operate, creating efficiencies, and opening doors to entirely new business possibilities.

Revolutionizing Industries with AI

The transformative power of AI lies in its ability to enhance efficiency, optimize resources, and enable smarter decision-making. India's industries are embracing AI to drive growth and innovation:

Healthcare: AI-powered diagnostic tools are enabling early detection of diseases like cancer and diabetes, improving patient outcomes. Startups such as **Niramai** are using AI for thermal imaging to detect breast cancer, while AI-driven apps provide virtual consultations and personalized health recommendations.

Manufacturing: AI is streamlining production processes by automating repetitive tasks and predicting equipment maintenance needs, reducing downtime and costs. In sectors like automotive and electronics, AI is enhancing precision and enabling the design of smarter, more efficient products.

Finance and Retail: AI algorithms are transforming retail by predicting consumer behavior and enabling personalized shopping experiences. In finance, AI-driven tools are improving fraud detection, automating loan approvals, and offering robo-advisory services for wealth management.

These innovations underscore how AI is driving efficiency and creating value across diverse industries, making it a cornerstone of India's economic transformation.

India as a Global AI Innovation Hub

India's strategic investments in AI research and development are positioning the country as a leader in global innovation.

Government Initiatives: Programs like **National AI Strategy** and **Digital India** are fostering the growth of AI technologies, encouraging startups and academic institutions to explore AI applications. The establishment of **AI research centers** and partnerships with global tech companies ensure India remains at the cutting edge of AI advancements.

Startups Driving Innovation: India's vibrant startup ecosystem includes AI-driven companies like **CureMetrix**, **Haptik**, and **Mad Street Den**, which are making strides in areas such as healthcare diagnostics, conversational AI, and visual intelligence. With access to large datasets and a skilled workforce, India's startups are developing solutions tailored to global markets.

Talent Advantage: India's vast pool of engineers and data scientists, coupled with its reputation for IT excellence, makes it an attractive destination for AI research and development. Collaboration between academic institutions and industries ensures a steady pipeline of talent ready to tackle AI challenges.

India's focus on fostering an innovation-driven ecosystem has cemented its status as a key player in the global AI landscape.

Applications Addressing India's Unique Challenges

One of AI's most compelling strengths lies in its ability to address challenges unique to India's diverse and complex environment:

Agriculture: AI is revolutionizing farming practices with tools that analyze soil health, predict weather patterns, and provide real-time crop management insights. AI-powered platforms are helping farmers optimize resource usage, reduce waste, and increase yields, contributing to greater food security.

Urban Planning: With India's rapid urbanization, AI is playing a crucial role in designing smarter cities. Applications include traffic management systems that reduce congestion, energy-efficient solutions for smart grids, and predictive analytics for infrastructure maintenance.

Personalized Medicine: AI is enabling the shift from generic healthcare solutions to personalized medicine tailored to individual genetic and lifestyle factors. Predictive models are helping identify high-risk patients, enabling preventive interventions that save lives and reduce healthcare costs.

These applications showcase AI's potential to not only advance industries but also improve the quality of life for millions across India.

Contributing to Global Advancements

India's AI-driven industries are not only addressing local challenges but are also contributing to global innovation:

Collaborative Research: Partnerships with global organizations and academic institutions are enabling knowledge exchange and joint development of AI technologies.

Scalable Solutions: India's expertise in creating cost-effective, scalable solutions ensures that its AI advancements can be deployed in other developing regions, bridging technology gaps worldwide.

Ethical AI Leadership: With a focus on ethical AI practices, India is actively shaping global discussions on responsible AI development and deployment.

The Road Ahead

As AI continues to evolve, its integration into India's industries will deepen, driving economic growth and societal progress. Investments in AI research, talent development, and innovation ecosystems will ensure India remains at the forefront of this revolution.

For businesses, policymakers, and innovators, India's AI journey offers a glimpse into a future where technology and human ingenuity combine to solve real-world problems, create opportunities, and shape a better tomorrow.

India's embrace of AI-driven industries signals not just the age of automation, but the dawn of intelligent solutions that promise to transform lives and economies across the globe.

Vision 2047: India's Centenary Goals as a Global Economic Powerhouse

As India nears its centenary of independence in 2047, it envisions a future that cements its position as a global economic and technological powerhouse. The vision is not just about achieving economic milestones but also about fostering innovation, ensuring sustainability, and creating an inclusive society that uplifts all its citizens. With clear goals and strategic pillars, India's Vision 2047 outlines a path to transformative growth, global leadership, and equitable development.

Economic Growth and Development

The cornerstone of Vision 2047 is India's ambition to become a **$40 trillion economy**, a goal that leverages the country's demographic and technological strengths.

Harnessing the Demographic Dividend: With a median age of 28 years, India boasts one of the youngest populations in the world. This youthful demographic represents a massive **productive workforce** poised to drive economic expansion. Investments in skill development, education, and job creation will ensure that this potential is fully realized. Programs like **Skill India** and **PMKVY (Pradhan Mantri Kaushal Vikas Yojana)** are designed to prepare India's youth for emerging industries and future job markets.

Infrastructure as a Growth Enabler: Vision 2047 places significant emphasis on **world-class infrastructure** to fuel economic growth. Projects like **Bharatmala** (road connectivity), **Sagarmala** (port development), and high-speed rail corridors will ensure seamless movement of goods and people, reducing logistics costs and enhancing productivity. **Smart cities** equipped with sustainable urban planning, efficient public transport, and green energy solutions will serve as hubs of innovation and economic activity.

Energy Security: India is focused on achieving energy security through diversified sources, including renewable energy and nuclear power. By 2047, India aims to reduce its reliance on fossil fuels and create a sustainable energy ecosystem that supports economic growth.

Global Leadership in Innovation

India's centenary vision is underpinned by its aspiration to lead the world in **knowledge-driven industries** such as biotechnology, space technology, and renewable energy.

Biotechnology Revolution: India is positioning itself as a hub for **biosimilars**, **genomics**, and **personalized medicine**, with significant investments in R&D. Collaborative efforts between academia and industry are fostering breakthroughs in healthcare, agriculture, and industrial applications, making India a global player in biotech innovation.

Space Technology: Building on the successes of missions like **Chandrayaan-3** and the **Aditya-L1 Solar Mission**, India aims to dominate the **commercial space sector** through satellite launches, interplanetary missions, and space tourism.

Initiatives to encourage private space startups, coupled with ISRO's advancements, will cement India's leadership in the global space economy.

Entrepreneurial Ecosystem: Programs like **Startup India** and **Digital India** are creating a fertile environment for entrepreneurship and technological innovation. By fostering **academic-industry collaborations** and providing funding for research, India is nurturing a vibrant ecosystem that can tackle global challenges with innovative solutions.

Sustainability and Inclusivity

Vision 2047 underscores the importance of aligning **economic growth** with **environmental sustainability** and **social inclusivity**, ensuring that progress benefits all sections of society.

Achieving Net-Zero Emissions: India is committed to reaching **net-zero emissions by 2070**, with interim targets focused on increasing renewable energy capacity and reducing carbon intensity. Programs like **National Hydrogen Mission** and **Renewable Energy Parks** aim to establish India as a leader in green energy while contributing to global efforts to combat climate change.

Reducing Inequality: Policies targeting **education**, **healthcare**, and **financial inclusion** are central to bridging socio-economic divides. Initiatives like **Ayushman Bharat** (universal health coverage) and **Jan Dhan Yojana** (financial inclusion) aim to empower marginalized communities and enhance their quality of life. The government's focus on **women's empowerment** and rural development ensures that growth is both inclusive and equitable.

Education as a Foundation: Strengthening the education system, particularly in science, technology, engineering, and mathematics (STEM), is a priority. Investments in higher education and vocational training will ensure India's workforce is prepared for the challenges of the future.

India's Path to 2047: Challenges and Opportunities

While Vision 2047 is ambitious, achieving it will require overcoming significant challenges:

Policy Consistency: Stable and clear policies will be essential to attract long-term investments and build investor confidence.

Technological Integration: Rapid advancements in AI, quantum computing, and automation must be integrated across industries to maintain competitiveness.

Global Collaboration: India must strengthen its partnerships with other nations, leveraging trade agreements and knowledge exchange to accelerate progress.

However, India's **resilience**, **entrepreneurial spirit**, and **youthful energy** provide a strong foundation to address these challenges and seize emerging opportunities.

In summary, Vision 2047 represents India's aspirations for a future where it emerges as a global economic and technological leader. With clear goals around economic growth, innovation, and sustainability, the nation is poised to create a transformative impact both domestically and globally.

As India moves toward its centenary of independence, its commitment to inclusivity, sustainability, and innovation will not only shape its destiny but also contribute to solving global challenges. For investors, innovators, and global partners, Vision 2047 offers a compelling opportunity to be part of a nation that is shaping the future while embracing its rich legacy of diversity, resilience, and progress.

The Role of Policy Reforms and Innovation in Shaping India's Future

Policy reforms and innovation are the dual engines propelling India toward its vision of global leadership. Together, they form the foundation for a dynamic, inclusive, and forward-looking economy capable of meeting the challenges and opportunities of the 21st century.

Policy Reforms: Unlocking India's Potential

India's economic transformation has been driven by a series of **proactive policy reforms** that create a conducive environment for growth, investment, and development.

Reforms in Taxation: The introduction of the **Goods and Services Tax (GST)** unified India's vast and diverse economy into a single market, reducing tax complexities and improving compliance. Ongoing efforts to streamline corporate taxation and rationalize indirect taxes continue to enhance India's appeal as an investment destination.

Modernizing Labor Laws: The consolidation of multiple labor laws into **four labor codes** has simplified compliance for businesses while ensuring worker protection and welfare. These reforms encourage **flexible hiring practices** and promote investments in labor-intensive industries like manufacturing and textiles.

Ease of Doing Business: India has made remarkable progress in improving its **Ease of Doing Business rankings**, moving up to the 63rd position globally by implementing reforms in areas such as starting a business, resolving insolvency, and obtaining construction permits. The **National Single Window System (NSWS)** is a digital initiative that provides businesses with a unified platform for obtaining licenses and clearances, further reducing bureaucratic hurdles.

Focus on Regional Development: Policies aimed at **balanced regional growth** are unlocking opportunities in Tier 2 and Tier 3 cities. Industrial corridors, rural development initiatives, and infrastructure upgrades are driving economic activity beyond urban centers.

Future policy reforms will emphasize **simplifying regulations**, strengthening **public-private partnerships (PPPs)**, and aligning governance with global best practices. By fostering a predictable and transparent policy environment, India is ensuring sustained economic momentum.

Innovation Ecosystem: Driving Growth Through Creativity

India's rise as a global leader in innovation is powered by its **vibrant startup culture**, strong academic institutions, and government-backed initiatives that prioritize technological advancements.

Startup India and Digital India: Programs like **Startup India** provide funding, tax benefits, and mentorship to entrepreneurs, fostering a culture of innovation and risk-taking. **Digital India** has accelerated the adoption of digital technologies, bridging the urban-rural divide and enabling access to e-governance, education, and healthcare services.

Collaborative Research and Development: Partnerships between academic institutions, industries, and government are driving breakthroughs in **green hydrogen**, **quantum computing**, and **advanced manufacturing technologies**. Institutions like **IITs** and research hubs such as **Indian Space Research Organisation (ISRO)** are spearheading innovation in critical areas, from renewable energy to space exploration.

Focus on Emerging Technologies: India is actively investing in **artificial intelligence (AI)**, **blockchain**, and **biotechnology**, with applications that range from precision agriculture to personalized medicine. The development of **smart cities** and **Industry 4.0** solutions further showcases India's commitment to technological advancement.

India's **innovation ecosystem** thrives on its ability to combine local ingenuity with global expertise, ensuring that the nation remains competitive in the fast-evolving global economy.

Global Collaborations: Strengthening India's International Ties

India's global ambitions are bolstered by strategic collaborations that facilitate knowledge exchange, technology transfer, and joint ventures in high-impact sectors.

High-Tech Partnerships: Collaborations with nations like the **United States, Japan**, and the **European Union** are driving advancements in areas such as **semiconductor manufacturing**, **clean energy**, and **defense technology**. India's participation in global initiatives like the **Quad Tech Network** and **International Solar Alliance** reflects its growing influence in shaping international technological and environmental agendas.

Trade Agreements and Global Forums: India's active role in **regional trade agreements** and participation in forums like **G20** and **BRICS** have solidified its position as a key player in global economic governance. Trade pacts focused on reducing tariffs, enhancing market access, and fostering innovation-driven industries are unlocking opportunities for Indian businesses abroad.

Knowledge Exchange: Joint research programs with global universities and R&D centers are enabling Indian scientists and entrepreneurs to collaborate on cutting-edge technologies.

India's growing integration into global supply chains and its ability to leverage international partnerships underscore its role as a leader in the global innovation ecosystem.

In conclusion, the synergy between policy reforms and innovation is shaping India's trajectory as a global powerhouse. Reforms in taxation, labor laws, and business regulations are creating a fertile ground for investment, while a thriving innovation ecosystem is driving technological advancements across industries.

Global collaborations further amplify India's potential, ensuring it remains a vital contributor to international economic and technological progress. With its forward-looking policies and unwavering focus on innovation, India is not only preparing for the challenges of the future but also positioning itself as a beacon of growth, resilience, and ingenuity on the global stage.

Conclusion

India stands at the crossroads of a transformative journey, driven by its capacity to **adapt, innovate, and lead** in industries that define the future. The nation's evolution from a rapidly growing economy to a global powerhouse is rooted in its ability to leverage technological advancements, implement forward-thinking policies, and maintain a steadfast commitment to **inclusive growth and sustainability**.

A Future Built on Innovation and Sustainability

India's rise is fueled by breakthroughs in sectors that hold the promise of shaping tomorrow's world.

Space Technology: From **Chandrayaan-3** to the flourishing private space ecosystem, India is charting a course that not only advances space exploration but also transforms industries like communication, agriculture, and disaster management.

AI-Driven Solutions: With artificial intelligence addressing challenges in healthcare, urban planning, and personalized medicine, India is positioning itself as a leader in cutting-edge innovation.

Fintech Revolution: Transformative platforms like **UPI** and advancements in digital lending and blockchain are democratizing financial services, making India a model for financial inclusion on a global scale.

These advancements highlight India's ability to blend **economic progress** with **societal and environmental goals**, creating solutions that are not only impactful but also sustainable.

Vision 2047: A Blueprint for Global Leadership

As India approaches its centenary of independence, **Vision 2047** serves as a roadmap for the country's transformation into a **global economic powerhouse**.

Economic Resilience: With a target of achieving a **$40 trillion economy**, Vision 2047 underscores India's focus on leveraging its **demographic dividend**, **infrastructure development**, and **technological prowess**.

Global Innovation Leadership: By prioritizing sectors like biotechnology, space technology, and renewable energy, India aims to lead the global transition to knowledge-driven industries.

Sustainability and Inclusivity: Vision 2047 envisions a future where economic growth is harmonized with environmental sustainability and societal equity, exemplifying a holistic approach to development.

Opportunities for Global Stakeholders

India's journey presents unparalleled opportunities for **investors, entrepreneurs, and global leaders**:

For Investors: The nation's diverse and rapidly evolving economy offers lucrative prospects across sectors, from emerging technologies to traditional industries reinvented for the modern age.

For Entrepreneurs: India's vibrant **startup ecosystem**, supported by government initiatives and a large, tech-savvy workforce, provides fertile ground for innovation and scaling.

For Global Leaders: Collaborating with India offers access to a market that is not only vast but also one that serves as a model for balancing growth with inclusion and sustainability.

Shaping the Trajectory of the 21st Century

India's future magnetism lies in its ability to turn challenges into opportunities, whether through bold reforms, pioneering innovation, or strategic global partnerships. The country's approach to development—anchored in resilience, ingenuity, and vision—ensures that it remains at the forefront of the global narrative.

For the world, India represents a partner in progress, a hub of innovation, and a leader in addressing shared challenges like climate change, digital transformation, and global economic stability.

As the 21st century unfolds, India's story is one of boundless potential and profound impact—a nation poised to **reshape the future and inspire generations to come**.

13. Practical Guide for Investors: How to Invest in India

India's dynamic economy offers a wealth of opportunities for investors, from established industries to emerging sectors like technology, renewable energy, and e-commerce. However, successfully entering and navigating the Indian market requires a well-informed and strategic approach. This chapter serves as a practical guide for investors, detailing the steps to establish a presence in India, the resources available for assistance, and the benefits of partnering with local businesses.

Step-by-Step Process for Entering India's Market

Entering India's vibrant and diverse market is an exciting opportunity, offering substantial rewards for businesses that approach it with a clear and methodical strategy. This step-by-step guide outlines how to navigate India's complexities and set a strong foundation for success.

1. Conduct Market Research

A thorough understanding of the market is the foundation for a successful entry.

Understand Sector Dynamics: Analyze the specific industry you are targeting, focusing on current demand trends, competitive landscapes, and regulatory frameworks. For example, sectors like technology, renewable energy, and healthcare are experiencing rapid growth and offer significant opportunities.

Identify Consumer Behavior: India's population is incredibly diverse, with varying preferences based on geography, income, and culture. Urban consumers often favor premium products and services, while rural markets prioritize affordability and utility.

Assess Regional Opportunities: Tier 2 and Tier 3 cities, such as Indore, Kochi, and Lucknow, are emerging as economic hubs with increasing disposable incomes and infrastructure investments. Conduct localized studies to identify untapped markets and tailor strategies accordingly.

2. Choose the Right Investment Structure

Your mode of entry should align with your business goals and risk appetite.

Wholly Owned Subsidiary: This structure provides complete control over operations, allowing you to implement global strategies without interference. Ideal for businesses with substantial resources and long-term plans in India.

Joint Venture: Partnering with a local entity can help navigate regulatory and cultural nuances. A joint venture allows access to established networks and reduces the initial investment burden. For example, Maruti Suzuki's joint venture has been a cornerstone of its success in India.

Branch Office/Representative Office: Establishing a branch office is a low-risk way to explore the market, test products, and build relationships before committing to full-scale operations.

3. Comply with Regulatory Requirements

Understanding and adhering to India's regulatory framework is essential to ensure smooth operations.

Understand FDI Policies:

India allows up to 100% Foreign Direct Investment (FDI) in most sectors, such as technology and manufacturing, while others, like retail, require prior government approval. Use resources like **Invest India** to stay updated on FDI guidelines.

Register Your Business: Register with the **Ministry of Corporate Affairs (MCA)**, obtain a Director Identification Number (DIN), and complete necessary filings. For specific industries, additional licenses may be required, such as environmental clearances for manufacturing units.

Tax and Legal Compliance: Familiarize yourself with India's tax structures, including **GST (Goods and Services Tax)**, corporate taxes, and any sector-specific levies. Ensure compliance with labor laws, especially if you plan to hire local talent.

4. Secure Funding and Banking Support

Setting up a robust financial structure is critical for smooth operations.

Open a Bank Account: Choose a financial institution registered with the Reserve Bank of India (RBI) to handle transactions and operational needs. Leading banks like **HDFC Bank, State Bank of India (SBI)**, and **ICICI Bank** offer business-friendly services tailored to foreign investors.

Explore Government Incentives: Many sectors, such as renewable energy and manufacturing, benefit from government subsidies and tax incentives. Programs like **Make in India** and **PLI (Production Linked Incentive) schemes** provide financial advantages to foreign businesses.

5. Establish Local Operations

Operational efficiency depends on how well you integrate into India's local ecosystem.

Hire Local Talent: Local employees understand regional cultures and consumer behaviors, helping businesses adapt effectively. Leverage India's vast talent pool, particularly in technology, finance, and manufacturing sectors.

Set Up Supply Chains: Establish supply chains tailored to India's infrastructure and logistical nuances. Collaborate with local distributors and suppliers to streamline operations and reduce costs.

6. Build Market Presence

Visibility and consumer engagement are key to success in India's competitive market.

Invest in Marketing Strategies: Utilize digital platforms like **Google Ads**, **Facebook**, and **regional social media** to target specific demographics. Develop multilingual campaigns to cater to India's linguistic diversity. For example, e-commerce players often launch promotions in Hindi, Tamil, and other regional languages.

Participate in Industry Events: Attend trade fairs, exhibitions, and business forums to build networks and showcase your brand. Events like the **India International Trade Fair** and **DefExpo** provide excellent platforms for connecting with stakeholders and consumers.

Thus, by following this structured approach, businesses can navigate the complexities of India's market and unlock its immense potential. With its diverse opportunities, supportive policies, and growing economy, India offers a fertile ground for investments across sectors.

Approach the journey with diligence, adaptability, and cultural sensitivity, and the Indian market can deliver significant returns on investment while positioning your business as a key player in one of the world's fastest-growing economies.

Key Resources: Government Bodies, Financial Institutions, and Trade Groups

India provides a robust ecosystem of support for investors, with dedicated government bodies, financial institutions, and trade associations that cater to the diverse needs of businesses entering the market. These resources play a critical role in guiding investors through regulatory processes, offering financial solutions, and creating opportunities for collaboration and growth.

Government Bodies: Enabling Investment Success

India's government has established several agencies and departments to facilitate and streamline investment processes, ensuring that investors can focus on growth while navigating the country's complexities with ease.

Invest India: As the national investment promotion agency, **Invest India** serves as a one-stop solution for all investor needs. It offers end-to-end support, including market research, site selection, and operational guidance. The agency also connects investors with relevant stakeholders and provides insights into sector-specific opportunities and government initiatives.

Department for Promotion of Industry and Internal Trade (DPIIT): DPIIT oversees policies related to foreign direct investment (FDI) and industrial growth. It provides guidance on incentives, sectoral reforms, and initiatives aimed at improving the **ease of doing business**. DPIIT plays a key role in formulating policies that align with India's economic goals, such as **Make in India** and **Startup India**.

State Investment Promotion Boards: Each Indian state has a dedicated **investment promotion board** that offers localized support to investors. These boards provide insights into region-specific opportunities, facilitate approvals and clearances, and offer incentives tailored to state priorities. For example, **Tamil Nadu Guidance Bureau** and **Gujarat Industrial Development Corporation (GIDC)** are known for their proactive investor engagement.

Financial Institutions: Tailored Solutions for Growth

India's financial ecosystem is well-equipped to meet the diverse funding and operational needs of investors, offering a range of banking and credit solutions.

Banks and Non-Banking Financial Companies (NBFCs): Major banks like the **State Bank of India (SBI)**, **HDFC Bank**, and **ICICI Bank** provide tailored financial services, including business loans, forex services, and trade finance solutions. NBFCs offer alternative credit options, especially for startups and small businesses, with simplified loan processes and flexible repayment structures.

Development Finance Institutions (DFIs): Institutions like the **Small Industries Development Bank of India (SIDBI)** focus on promoting micro, small, and medium enterprises (MSMEs). They provide credit support, equity funding, and mentoring services, particularly for businesses in emerging and underserved sectors. DFIs are instrumental in channeling resources to sectors like renewable energy, infrastructure, and agri-tech.

Venture Capital and Private Equity Support: India has a thriving venture capital ecosystem, with domestic and international funds actively investing in high-growth sectors like technology, healthcare, and e-commerce. Initiatives like **Fund of Funds for Startups (FFS)**, managed by SIDBI, provide financial support to early-stage startups.

Trade Groups and Industry Associations: Building Networks and Insights

Trade groups and industry associations play a crucial role in connecting investors with opportunities, offering industry insights, and fostering partnerships across sectors.

Confederation of Indian Industry (CII): CII is a leading industry association that provides a platform for dialogue between the government and businesses. It organizes events, trade fairs, and policy discussions, facilitating collaboration and networking among industry leaders.

Federation of Indian Chambers of Commerce and Industry (FICCI): FICCI supports businesses across sectors by offering market intelligence, policy advocacy, and networking opportunities. It works closely with international trade bodies to promote bilateral trade and investment.

NASSCOM: Representing India's IT and software services sector, NASSCOM provides guidance and support for tech-focused investors. It helps companies navigate the tech landscape, connect with talent pools, and adopt global best practices.

ASSOCHAM and PHD Chamber of Commerce: These associations cater to a wide range of industries, providing platforms for engagement, advocacy, and capacity building.

In short, India's well-established network of government bodies, financial institutions, and trade associations ensures that investors have access to the resources they need at every stage of their journey. Whether it's navigating regulatory requirements, securing financial support, or building industry connections, these resources form a vital backbone for investment success.

For investors seeking to tap into India's dynamic economy, leveraging these resources can streamline market entry, mitigate risks, and unlock opportunities across one of the world's most promising markets. By engaging with these institutions and associations, businesses can build a strong foundation for growth, innovation, and long-term success in India.

Insights into Partnering with Local Businesses

Partnering with local businesses is a strategic approach that has proven to be a game-changer for international investors looking to establish a foothold in India. The complexity of India's regulatory environment, cultural diversity, and regional market dynamics makes local collaboration a valuable tool for overcoming challenges and maximizing opportunities. Here's an expanded look at the key advantages of collaborating with local businesses.

1. Navigating Regulatory Landscapes

India's regulatory environment can be complex, with variations across sectors and states.

Expertise in Compliance: Local businesses are well-versed in navigating India's legal and regulatory framework, ensuring faster clearances and compliance with sector-specific requirements. They bring in-depth knowledge of processes such as registering with the Ministry of Corporate Affairs (MCA), obtaining sectoral licenses, and adhering to labor and tax regulations.

Reducing Delays and Risks: By partnering with local entities, international investors can avoid procedural delays and minimize the risk of non-compliance, which could otherwise disrupt operations. For example, local partners can handle state-specific regulations for industries like real estate and manufacturing, streamlining the approval process.

2. Cultural and Market Insights

India's cultural diversity and varied consumer behaviors can pose challenges for foreign investors unfamiliar with regional nuances.

Understanding Local Preferences: Indian businesses provide invaluable insights into consumer preferences, helping foreign companies tailor products and services to meet local demands. For instance, food and beverage brands often adapt their offerings to suit regional tastes, as McDonald's India did by introducing menu items like the McAloo Tikki Burger.

Regional Expertise: With distinct markets across states and cities, local partners help identify regional trends, enabling targeted marketing and efficient resource allocation. They can also guide international firms on pricing strategies, packaging preferences, and promotional tactics that resonate with Indian consumers.

3. Established Networks

Building distribution networks, supplier relationships, and a customer base from scratch can be time-intensive and expensive. Local partnerships offer a faster, more efficient alternative.

Pre-Existing Distribution Channels: Local partners bring established supply chains and distribution networks, ensuring seamless market entry. This advantage is particularly significant in sectors like FMCG and retail, where speed and efficiency in distribution can determine success.

Supplier Relationships: Indian partners often have long-standing relationships with suppliers, enabling better pricing, quality assurance, and supply chain reliability. For example, IKEA partnered with local vendors to source materials, meeting India's FDI requirements while building a robust supply chain.

4. Joint Ventures and Collaborations

Joint ventures and collaborations are a popular entry strategy for global companies seeking to leverage local expertise and resources.

Examples of Success: **Walmart-Flipkart**: Walmart's acquisition of Flipkart allowed it to enter India's e-commerce market by leveraging Flipkart's local expertise, consumer insights, and supply chain infrastructure.

Maruti Suzuki: Suzuki's joint venture with Maruti revolutionized India's automobile market, combining affordable pricing with locally tailored models.

Expanding Market Footprint: Through collaborations, international investors can tap into existing consumer bases and scale operations faster.

Local partners also play a pivotal role in navigating competitive landscapes by leveraging their market position and reputation.

5. Risk Mitigation

Entering a new market always comes with uncertainties. Collaborating with local businesses can help mitigate operational and financial risks.

Shared Responsibility: Local partners share the risks associated with compliance, market entry, and operations, reducing the burden on international investors. They are better equipped to address region-specific challenges, such as political instability or local economic slowdowns.

Adaptability to Market Dynamics: Local businesses are often more attuned to changing market dynamics, enabling faster decision-making and adaptation. For example, during the COVID-19 pandemic, many local partnerships helped foreign investors pivot their strategies to address supply chain disruptions and shifting consumer behavior.

In summary, collaborating with local businesses offers international investors a strategic advantage in navigating India's diverse and dynamic market. From regulatory compliance and cultural insights to pre-existing networks and risk sharing, these partnerships can significantly enhance the chances of success.

By forging strong relationships with trusted local entities, investors can not only accelerate market entry but also build a sustainable presence in India's thriving economy. The stories of successful collaborations, such as those of Walmart-Flipkart and Maruti Suzuki, highlight the transformative power of local partnerships in unlocking India's immense potential. For businesses entering India, partnering locally is not just an option—it's often the key to long-term growth and success.

Best Practices for Partnerships

Forming a partnership in India can be a transformative strategy for international investors, but the success of such collaborations depends on implementing effective practices. By focusing on due diligence, establishing clear agreements, and fostering trust, businesses can lay the foundation for a mutually beneficial relationship. Here's an expanded look at the best practices for partnerships in India.

1. Conduct Due Diligence to Identify Reliable and Reputable Partners

Choosing the right partner is the cornerstone of any successful collaboration.

Evaluate Business Credentials: Assess the partner's financial stability, operational history, and market reputation. Look for businesses with a proven track record in their respective industries. Verify certifications, licenses, and compliance with local laws to ensure the partner operates within the regulatory framework.

Analyze Market Fit: Ensure the partner's capabilities align with your business goals. For instance, a company with a robust distribution network is essential for retail or FMCG sectors, while a technology partner should demonstrate expertise in innovation and R&D.

Leverage Third-Party Resources: Engage professional firms or consultants to conduct background checks and market research. Organizations like **Invest India** and **state investment boards** can also provide guidance in identifying trustworthy partners.

Assess Cultural Alignment: A partner's understanding of local cultural nuances and business practices is vital for smooth collaboration. Their ability to navigate India's diverse markets should align with your strategic vision.

2. Establish Clear Agreements Outlining Roles, Responsibilities, and Revenue-Sharing Models

A transparent and well-documented agreement is critical for avoiding misunderstandings and ensuring the partnership operates smoothly.

Define Roles and Responsibilities: Clearly delineate the roles of each partner, specifying operational duties, decision-making authority, and management structures. For example, if one partner handles supply chain logistics while the other focuses on marketing, these roles should be explicitly defined in the agreement.

Set Financial Terms: Outline revenue-sharing models, profit distribution, and cost-sharing mechanisms to avoid disputes. Specify how investments, operating expenses, and returns will be managed, including timelines for payments and reinvestments.

Include Exit Clauses: Establish terms for dissolving the partnership if needed, including procedures for asset division, intellectual property rights, and handling ongoing contracts. Exit strategies ensure that both parties have a clear understanding of their rights and obligations in case the partnership doesn't go as planned.

Legal Safeguards: Consult legal experts to draft the agreement, ensuring it complies with Indian laws and regulations. Incorporate clauses that address dispute resolution, arbitration, and confidentiality.

3. Invest in Building Strong Relationships: Trust and Collaboration are Key

The success of a partnership in India often depends on the strength of the relationship between the collaborating entities.

Prioritize Communication: Regular and open communication helps build trust and ensures alignment on goals and strategies. Schedule frequent check-ins to review performance, discuss challenges, and explore new opportunities. Use technology platforms to facilitate seamless communication, especially for international collaborations.

Foster Cultural Sensitivity: Respecting cultural values, traditions, and business etiquette is essential for building rapport. For example, understanding the importance of relationship-building and long-term commitments in Indian business culture can strengthen the partnership.

Collaborate on Strategic Goals: Align on long-term objectives, such as market expansion, revenue targets, or product innovation. Shared goals ensure both partners remain committed to the success of the venture.

Support Capacity Building: Invest in training and development programs for the partner's workforce to enhance operational efficiency and innovation. Capacity building demonstrates a commitment to the partnership's success.

Celebrate Milestones: Recognize and celebrate achievements, such as hitting revenue targets or successfully launching a product. This fosters goodwill and motivates both parties to continue working towards shared goals.

Thus, establishing a successful partnership in India requires more than just a formal agreement—it calls for careful planning, open communication, and a shared vision. By conducting thorough due diligence, setting clear expectations through detailed agreements, and fostering trust through collaboration, businesses can create partnerships that are resilient, adaptive, and mutually beneficial.

In India's dynamic market, partnerships that prioritize these best practices can unlock significant opportunities, enabling international investors to navigate complexities while achieving sustainable growth and long-term success.

Conclusion

Investing in India is more than just entering a market—it's embarking on a transformative journey in one of the world's most dynamic economies. The country's vast and diverse landscape, coupled with its burgeoning consumer base, robust industrial ecosystem, and forward-thinking policies, creates a fertile ground for global investors seeking growth, innovation, and impact.

A Strategic Approach to Success

India's market offers immense opportunities, but realizing its full potential requires a well-planned and strategic approach. Investors who dedicate time to understanding the complexities of the Indian economy—its regulatory environment, cultural nuances, and regional diversities—are better equipped to navigate challenges and capitalize on opportunities.

Leverage Institutional Support: Government bodies like **Invest India**, financial institutions such as **SIDBI**, and trade associations like **CII** provide critical resources and guidance for foreign investors. These entities simplify the process of entering and scaling in India, ensuring a smoother transition into the market.

The Role of Partnerships: Collaborating with local businesses and stakeholders is often the key to success. Such partnerships offer access to established networks, regional insights, and operational expertise, allowing foreign investors to integrate seamlessly into India's dynamic economy.

India: A Thriving Ecosystem

India is not merely a destination for capital—it is a vibrant ecosystem where challenges evolve into opportunities and innovation drives growth.

Challenges as Opportunities: While bureaucratic hurdles and regulatory complexities may initially seem daunting, they have also inspired reforms and innovation, creating a business environment that rewards resilience and adaptability.

A Diverse Market: India's unique diversity offers unparalleled opportunities for businesses across sectors, from traditional industries like agriculture and manufacturing to cutting-edge fields such as fintech, space technology, and artificial intelligence.

Innovation Hub: The rise of startups, fueled by government initiatives like **Startup India**, and advancements in emerging technologies position India as a global hub for innovation. Investors can benefit not just from India's consumer market but also from its thriving ecosystem of creators, innovators, and entrepreneurs.

Why India?

India's appeal as an investment destination is rooted in its ability to combine growth with inclusivity and sustainability.

Economic Resilience: Even amidst global uncertainties, India's economy has demonstrated remarkable resilience, maintaining steady growth driven by domestic demand and strategic reforms.

Policy-Driven Growth: Initiatives such as **Make in India**, **Digital India**, and **PLI schemes** underscore the government's commitment to fostering a business-friendly environment.

A Global Powerhouse in the Making: As the country moves toward its centenary goals under **Vision 2047**, it is setting the stage to emerge as one of the world's leading economic powerhouses, offering unparalleled potential for investors to contribute and thrive.

A Call to Global Investors

For global investors, India represents more than just a lucrative market—it is an opportunity to be part of an economic transformation that is shaping the trajectory of the 21st century. With its growing economy, vibrant culture of innovation, and a consumer base that is both vast and diverse, India stands out as one of the most compelling and rewarding investment destinations in the world.

Whether you are a multinational corporation, a tech entrepreneur, or an institutional investor, India offers the promise of growth, collaboration, and impact. By embracing India's challenges as opportunities and its complexities as strengths, investors can forge a path to sustainable success in one of the world's most promising markets.

India is not just a destination—it's a partnership, a journey, and an unparalleled opportunity to be part of a dynamic and thriving future.

14. Investment Opportunities in India's Stock Market

India's stock market is more than just a platform for trading equities; it is a reflection of the country's economic vitality, innovation, and future potential. As one of the fastest-growing financial markets globally, India offers opportunities across a spectrum of industries, from established conglomerates to emerging midcap companies and government enterprises. For global leaders and investors, the stock market represents a unique entry point to participate in and benefit from India's growth trajectory.

This chapter delves into the structure of India's stock market, key investment opportunities, and curated suggestions for companies that embody India's dynamic growth story.

1. Overview of India's Financial Markets

India's stock market is a cornerstone of its economic infrastructure, serving as a barometer of the nation's financial health and a gateway for domestic and international investors. Operating through two primary exchanges, the Indian stock market combines rich history with cutting-edge technology to cater to a diverse investor base.

Bombay Stock Exchange (BSE): Asia's Oldest Stock Exchange

Historical Significance: Established in 1875, the BSE holds the distinction of being Asia's first stock exchange. Over the decades, it has evolved from an open-outcry system to a fully electronic trading platform, maintaining its relevance in the modern era.

Diverse Listings: With over 5,000 listed companies, the BSE hosts a variety of businesses, ranging from large-cap giants to small and medium enterprises (SMEs). This diversity makes it a unique platform for investors seeking exposure to India's expansive economic spectrum.

Benchmark Index: The **Sensex**, BSE's flagship index comprising 30 of the largest and most actively traded companies, serves as a key indicator of market trends and investor sentiment in India.

National Stock Exchange (NSE): A Technology-Driven Powerhouse

Modern Trading Ecosystem: Established in 1992, the NSE introduced electronic trading to India, revolutionizing the market with speed, efficiency, and transparency.

Key Indices: The **Nifty50**, NSE's benchmark index comprising 50 blue-chip companies, reflects the performance of various sectors and is a popular choice for passive investors and global funds.

Market Leadership: NSE dominates trading volumes in India, thanks to its advanced technology, user-friendly interface, and a strong focus on investor education.

A Thriving Capital Market

India's stock market has witnessed remarkable growth in recent years, supported by robust economic fundamentals and structural reforms. As of 2024, the combined market capitalization of the BSE and NSE exceeds $3.7 trillion, placing India among the top 10 stock markets globally.

Retail Participation: The rise of digital trading platforms like Zerodha, Groww, and Upstox has democratized market access, attracting millions of first-time investors.

Foreign Investment: With simplified Foreign Portfolio Investment (FPI) regulations, India has become a favored destination for global capital, especially in sectors like technology, financial services, and healthcare.

Innovative Platforms: Initiatives like the **India International Exchange (INX)** at GIFT City offer seamless trading in international currencies, commodities, and equities, further integrating India into the global financial system.

Why It Matters

The Indian stock market is more than a financial marketplace—it is a reflection of the nation's growth story, innovation, and resilience. From facilitating wealth creation for millions to funding ambitious corporate expansions, the market plays a pivotal role in shaping India's economic destiny.

For investors, India's financial markets represent not just an opportunity to generate returns but also a chance to be part of a transformative journey that aligns with the aspirations of one of the world's fastest-growing economies.

2. Investment Avenues in India's Stock Market

India's stock market provides a wide array of investment opportunities that cater to diverse investor profiles, from risk-averse individuals seeking stable returns to aggressive investors aiming for high growth. Here's a detailed look at the key investment avenues:

Large-Cap Companies: Stability and Consistent Performance

Large-cap companies represent established players in the market, characterized by stability, robust business models, and reliable returns.

Why Invest? Large-cap stocks are ideal for investors looking for lower volatility and steady growth over the long term. These companies typically have a strong market presence, high liquidity, and the ability to weather economic downturns.

Key Players:

Reliance Industries: A diversified conglomerate with interests in energy, telecom, and retail, contributing significantly to India's GDP.

Tata Consultancy Services (TCS): A global IT services leader with a consistent track record of delivering shareholder value.

HDFC Bank: Known for its strong retail banking operations and innovative financial services.

Midcap and Emerging Companies: High Growth Potential

Midcap companies lie between the stability of large caps and the aggressive growth of small caps, offering a balance of risk and reward.

Why Invest? These companies often represent sectors or industries experiencing rapid growth, making them attractive for investors seeking capital appreciation.

Key Players:

L&T Technology Services (LTTS): A leader in engineering services, leveraging cutting-edge technologies like AI and IoT.

Narayana Hrudayalaya: A pioneer in affordable healthcare, meeting the needs of India's growing population.

RateGain Travel Tech: A rising star in travel technology, providing AI-driven solutions for the hospitality and tourism sectors.

Government-Owned Enterprises (PSUs): Strategic and Reliable Investments

Public Sector Undertakings (PSUs) are companies owned and operated by the government, often occupying strategic positions in critical sectors like energy, defense, and infrastructure.

Why Invest? PSUs are known for their dividend yields, stability, and role in nation-building, making them appealing to conservative investors.

Key Players:

Coal India: The world's largest coal producer, pivotal to India's energy sector.

Bharat Electronics Limited (BEL): A major player in defense electronics, benefiting from India's push for self-reliance in defense.

Hindustan Aeronautics Limited (HAL): A leader in aerospace manufacturing, contributing to India's growing export potential in defense.

Exchange-Traded Funds (ETFs): Low-Cost Diversification

ETFs offer an efficient way to invest in a basket of stocks, tracking indices or specific themes.

Why Invest? ETFs are ideal for passive investors seeking market exposure without the need for active management. They provide diversification, liquidity, and cost efficiency.

Popular Options:

Nifty50 ETF: Tracks the top 50 companies listed on the NSE, offering broad market exposure.

Sectoral ETFs: Focus on themes like banking, IT, or renewable energy for targeted investments.

Gold ETFs: Allow investors to participate in gold's price movements without owning physical gold.

Debt and Fixed Income: Stability and Regular Returns

For risk-averse investors, debt instruments like bonds and fixed-income securities offer a secure and predictable income stream.

Why Invest? These options are less volatile than equities, making them suitable for preserving capital while earning steady returns.

Key Instruments:

Corporate Bonds: Issued by companies to fund operations, offering higher returns than government bonds with moderate risk.

Government Securities (G-Secs): Long-term instruments backed by the Indian government, ensuring high safety.

Tax-Free Bonds: Ideal for high-net-worth individuals seeking tax-efficient income.

Why India's Stock Market is Attractive

India's financial markets are uniquely positioned to cater to both conservative and aggressive investment strategies. From stable dividends of PSUs to the high growth potential of midcap companies and the cost-efficient diversification of ETFs, the opportunities are vast and varied.

This diversity ensures that investors of all profiles, whether domestic or international, can find suitable options aligned with their goals, making India a global magnet for stock market investments.

3. Suggested Companies for Global Investors

India's stock market offers a plethora of opportunities for global investors, ranging from large-cap stalwarts to midcap growth stories and promising public sector undertakings. These companies represent a cross-section of India's vibrant economic landscape, reflecting its innovation, resilience, and growth potential.

Large-Cap Leaders

Large-cap companies, characterized by their stability and consistent performance, are the backbone of India's stock market. These firms offer reliable returns and are often the first choice for international investors.

Reliance Industries: A diversified conglomerate with significant interests in energy, petrochemicals, telecom (Jio), and retail.

A leader in renewable energy initiatives, particularly green hydrogen production.

TCS and Infosys: **TCS**: The largest IT services provider in India, excelling in digital transformation, cloud computing, and AI solutions.

Infosys: Renowned for its innovation in IT and consulting, with a strong global presence and cutting-edge services.

HDFC Bank: India's most valuable private sector bank, known for its innovative financial products and efficient operations.

A benchmark for stability in the Indian banking sector.

ICICI Bank: A leader in retail and corporate banking, offering innovative digital banking solutions.

Adani Enterprises: A rapidly growing conglomerate involved in infrastructure, renewable energy, and logistics, driving India's sustainable development goals.

Wipro: An IT and consulting giant, specializing in digital transformation and cloud solutions for global enterprises.

Bharti Airtel: A telecom leader with a strong foothold in mobile services, broadband, and enterprise solutions.

Actively investing in 5G and digital innovations.

Midcap Stars with Growth Potential

Midcap companies often represent high-growth sectors and emerging opportunities, making them ideal for investors seeking capital appreciation.

L&T Technology Services (LTTS): A leader in engineering services with expertise in Industry 4.0, smart manufacturing, and IoT solutions.

Narayana Hrudayalaya: A healthcare pioneer focusing on affordable cardiac care and hospital services, addressing India's growing medical needs.

Praj Industries: Innovating in bioenergy and renewable fuels, contributing to India's sustainability and clean energy goals.

Saksoft: A rapidly growing IT company specializing in digital transformation and data analytics.

RateGain Travel Technologies: Providing AI-driven solutions for the travel and hospitality sectors, capitalizing on the post-pandemic tourism boom.

Deepak Nitrite: A chemical manufacturing leader, benefiting from global demand for specialty chemicals and intermediates.

Zomato: A food delivery and technology company revolutionizing India's urban lifestyle and logistics ecosystem.

Promising Public Sector Undertakings (PSUs)

Public Sector Undertakings (PSUs) play a vital role in India's strategic sectors, offering stable returns and significant growth potential.

Coal India: The world's largest coal producer, essential for India's energy needs and industrial operations.

Bharat Electronics Limited (BEL): A defense electronics major, contributing to India's self-reliance in military technology.

Hindustan Aeronautics Limited (HAL): A key aerospace manufacturer, developing indigenous fighter aircraft and helicopters for India's defense forces.

Power Grid Corporation of India Limited: A leader in power transmission, ensuring efficient energy distribution across the country.

Indian Oil Corporation (IOC): The largest oil refining and marketing company in India, crucial for energy security and export growth.

NTPC Limited: India's largest power generation company, diversifying into renewable energy projects like solar and wind.

GAIL (India) Limited: A leader in natural gas production and distribution, aligning with India's push for clean energy.

Why These Companies Matter

Diversified Exposure: These companies provide access to a wide range of industries, from technology and finance to healthcare and energy.

Resilience: Many of these firms have proven their ability to thrive in dynamic economic conditions, offering a stable foundation for investment.

Innovation and Sustainability: Midcap stars and PSUs are driving innovation in emerging technologies and sustainable practices, aligning with global trends.

For global investors, these companies represent the pillars of India's growth story, offering a mix of stability, growth potential, and resilience. Whether you're seeking long-term investments or exploring high-growth opportunities, this curated list serves as a comprehensive guide to participating in one of the world's most dynamic economies.

4. The Role of Government Policies

India's government policies have played a pivotal role in creating a dynamic and investor-friendly stock market. By implementing reforms and incentives, the government has not only attracted foreign capital but also nurtured domestic growth, ensuring that the financial markets remain robust and resilient. Here's a closer look at how key policies are shaping India's stock market and investment landscape:

Foreign Portfolio Investment (FPI): Simplifying Global Participation

Foreign Portfolio Investment (FPI) is a cornerstone of India's integration into the global financial system.

Streamlined Processes: The Indian government, through the **Securities and Exchange Board of India (SEBI)**, has introduced simplified and transparent FPI registration processes. This encourages foreign investors to actively participate in equities, bonds, and derivatives.

Open Market Access: Up to 100% foreign investment is allowed in several sectors, including infrastructure, renewable energy, and IT, making India one of the most open economies for portfolio investments.

FPI Trends: Sectors like banking, IT, healthcare, and consumer goods have been major beneficiaries of FPI, with steady inflows reflecting global investor confidence.

Production Linked Incentive (PLI) Schemes: Catalyzing Manufacturing Growth

Introduced to boost domestic manufacturing and reduce import dependency, the **PLI Schemes** are transforming India into a global manufacturing hub.

Targeted Sectors: The PLI schemes focus on high-potential industries such as electronics, automotive, pharmaceuticals, renewable energy, and textiles, ensuring sector-specific growth.

Incentives for Investors: Companies achieving incremental production targets receive financial incentives, making India an attractive destination for both domestic and foreign manufacturers.

Impact on Stock Market: Key beneficiaries of the PLI schemes, like Tata Motors (electric vehicles), Dr. Reddy's Laboratories (pharmaceuticals), and Adani Green Energy (renewables), have seen increased investor interest and robust stock performance.

Ease of Doing Business Reforms: Building Investor Confidence

India's rank in the **Ease of Doing Business Index** has improved significantly, thanks to government-led reforms aimed at reducing red tape and fostering a pro-business environment.

Simplified Regulations: The introduction of the **National Single Window System (NSWS)** allows businesses to apply for multiple clearances through a unified portal, expediting approvals and reducing compliance burdens.

Taxation Reforms: Implementation of **Goods and Services Tax (GST)** has unified India into a single market, simplifying indirect taxation.

Reduction in corporate tax rates (22% for domestic companies and 15% for new manufacturing firms) has bolstered corporate profitability and attracted investments.

Labor Law Reforms: Consolidation of 29 labor laws into four labor codes has introduced flexibility in hiring, reduced compliance costs, and fostered a conducive environment for businesses.

Impact on Investments: These reforms have improved investor confidence, leading to a steady rise in domestic and foreign investments across sectors like real estate, infrastructure, and technology.

Digital India and Financial Market Integration

The government's **Digital India** initiative has significantly enhanced the efficiency and accessibility of the financial markets.

E-KYC and Online Trading: Digitized Know Your Customer (KYC) processes have made it easier for individuals and institutional investors to open trading accounts and access stock markets.

Market Transparency: The adoption of blockchain and AI-driven technologies ensures transparency in trading and regulatory compliance, increasing trust among investors.

Focused Policies for Retail Investor Growth

Systematic Investment Plans (SIPs): Encouraged by tax incentives under **Section 80C**, SIPs have seen record monthly inflows, reflecting growing retail participation.

Investor Protection: SEBI has implemented stringent norms to safeguard investor interests, including mandatory disclosures and grievance redressal mechanisms.

Why These Policies Matter to Investors

India's policy-driven reforms have created a robust foundation for its stock market, ensuring it remains competitive, transparent, and attractive to a diverse investor base. Whether it's the incentivization of manufacturing under the PLI schemes or the simplified processes for foreign portfolio investors, these policies collectively ensure that India's financial markets are poised for sustained growth.

For global and domestic investors alike, India's policy framework is a testament to its commitment to fostering a vibrant, resilient, and forward-looking investment ecosystem.

5. Rising Retail Participation

India's stock market has experienced a significant surge in retail participation, marking a transformative shift in how individuals engage with equities, mutual funds, and other investment instruments. This phenomenon is driven by technological advancements, innovative investment options, and a growing culture of financial awareness. Retail investors now play a crucial role in shaping market dynamics, adding resilience and depth to the Indian financial ecosystem.

Technology Platforms: Democratizing Investments

The advent of technology-driven platforms has revolutionized stock market access, bringing trading to the fingertips of millions of Indians.

Accessibility and User-Friendly Interfaces: Apps like Angle One, IIFL, **Zerodha**, **Groww**, **Upstox**, and **many other** have simplified the investment process with intuitive interfaces, minimal documentation, and affordable pricing structures.

Low-Cost Trading: These platforms offer zero or minimal brokerage fees, attracting first-time investors who may have been deterred by traditional trading costs.

Real-Time Data and Insights: Retail investors benefit from comprehensive research tools, live market data, and performance trackers integrated into these platforms, enabling informed decision-making.

Rise of Millennial Investors: A significant portion of new retail participants are millennials and Gen Z individuals who prefer the convenience of mobile-first platforms and digital investments.

Systematic Investment Plans (SIPs): Fostering a Disciplined Approach

Systematic Investment Plans (SIPs) have emerged as a preferred investment tool among Indian retail investors, offering a structured and disciplined approach to wealth creation.

Monthly Inflows: SIP contributions reached record levels in 2024, with monthly inflows surpassing ₹15,000 crore, reflecting the growing confidence of retail investors in mutual funds.

Rupee Cost Averaging: By investing a fixed amount regularly, SIPs help investors mitigate market volatility and build a diversified portfolio over time.

Tax Benefits: Many SIP investments qualify for tax deductions under Section 80C, adding to their appeal among salaried individuals.

Financial Security: SIPs are particularly popular for long-term goals like retirement planning, children's education, and home purchases, encouraging a culture of financial preparedness.

Financial Literacy: Empowering First-Time Investors

The rise in retail participation can also be attributed to the increasing emphasis on financial literacy and awareness campaigns.

Educational Initiatives: Organizations like **NSE Academy** and **BSE Institute** offer courses on stock market basics, technical analysis, and personal finance management, catering to diverse learning needs.

Social Media and Influencers: Platforms like YouTube, Instagram, and Twitter are now filled with content creators and financial influencers who simplify complex investment concepts, making them relatable and actionable.

Government Campaigns: Initiatives like **Investor Awareness Programs (IAPs)** by SEBI aim to educate the masses about investment opportunities, rights, and risks.

Community Learning: Online forums and discussion groups enable retail investors to share insights, strategies, and experiences, fostering a collaborative investment environment.

The Shift in Retail Investor Behavior

Rise of DIY Investing: A growing number of investors are opting for a do-it-yourself (DIY) approach, relying on research and insights from digital platforms rather than traditional financial advisors.

Diversification Across Asset Classes: Retail investors are exploring a mix of equities, mutual funds, ETFs, and fixed-income instruments, reflecting a nuanced understanding of risk and returns.

Focus on Long-Term Goals: Unlike earlier trends of speculative trading, today's retail investors are more focused on long-term wealth creation, driven by a better understanding of market dynamics.

Impact on India's Stock Market

The surge in retail participation has transformed India's financial landscape:

Market Depth: The influx of retail investors has increased liquidity and stabilized market performance, particularly during volatile periods.

Broader Ownership: A diversified investor base reduces market concentration, ensuring that a wide range of industries and sectors benefit from increased investments.

Democratization of Wealth Creation: The participation of small-scale investors in equity markets is bridging wealth disparities, enabling broader societal growth.

Why Rising Retail Participation Matters

India's stock market is no longer the domain of institutional investors alone. The rise of retail participation has brought a wave of democratization, empowering individuals to take control of their financial futures.

This trend reflects a maturing financial ecosystem, where technology, education, and innovation converge to create opportunities for millions. For global investors and leaders, this signifies a robust, resilient market that thrives on the active engagement of its people.

6. Opportunities in Key Sectors

India's growth story is deeply intertwined with its robust and dynamic sectors that not only address domestic needs but also make a significant impact on global markets. Each sector offers unique investment opportunities and represents the country's potential as a global powerhouse. Here's an expanded view of key sectors driving India's economy:

Information Technology and Digital Transformation

India's IT industry is a cornerstone of its economic success, with global players and emerging companies driving innovation in digital transformation.

Leading Companies:

Tata Consultancy Services (TCS) and **Infosys**: These giants have a strong global presence, delivering cutting-edge solutions in AI, cloud computing, and blockchain to Fortune 500 companies.

L&T Technology Services (LTTS): A leader in engineering services, LTTS specializes in Industry 4.0 solutions, including IoT-enabled smart factories and automation systems.

Opportunities:

AI and Machine Learning: India is becoming a hub for AI-driven innovation, transforming industries such as healthcare, finance, and retail.

Cybersecurity and Blockchain: Increasing digitalization has led to a surge in demand for robust cybersecurity frameworks and blockchain solutions.

Global Impact: India accounts for over 55% of the global outsourcing market, showcasing its dominance in IT services and digital solutions.

Healthcare and Pharmaceuticals

India's healthcare and pharmaceutical sectors are globally renowned for their affordability, innovation, and scale.

Leading Companies:

Sun Pharma: A leading manufacturer of generic medicines, catering to markets in over 100 countries.

Cipla: Known for its affordable treatments for respiratory, cardiovascular, and oncology ailments.

Dr. Reddy's Laboratories: A key player in biosimilars and specialty medications, addressing global health challenges.

Opportunities:

Generic Drug Exports: India is the largest exporter of generic drugs, with a 20% share of the global market.

MedTech and Biotech: The medtech sector is experiencing rapid growth, driven by innovations in diagnostics, wearable devices, and robotic surgery.

Medical Tourism: High-quality healthcare services at affordable costs make India a preferred destination for medical tourism, projected to contribute $13 billion annually by 2025.

Global Impact: India's pharmaceutical exports, including vaccines, are instrumental in addressing global health crises, such as the COVID-19 pandemic.

Renewable Energy and Sustainability

India's commitment to sustainable development is creating vast opportunities in renewable energy and green technologies.

Leading Companies:

Adani Green Energy: A pioneer in solar and wind power projects, contributing significantly to India's renewable capacity.

Tata Power: Diversifying into solar rooftops, EV charging infrastructure, and energy efficiency solutions.

NTPC: Expanding its portfolio to include green hydrogen and offshore wind energy projects.

Opportunities:

Solar and Wind Power: India aims to achieve 500 GW of renewable energy capacity by 2030, presenting opportunities for investments in solar parks and wind farms.

Green Hydrogen: As a clean energy source, green hydrogen is poised to revolutionize industries such as transportation and heavy manufacturing.

Energy Storage: Innovations in battery storage and grid management are critical to enhancing renewable energy efficiency.

Global Impact: India ranks among the top five countries globally in installed renewable energy capacity, setting benchmarks for sustainable energy transitions.

Defense and Aerospace

India's defense and aerospace sectors are undergoing a transformative phase, with a strong emphasis on indigenous manufacturing and export growth.

Leading Companies:

Hindustan Aeronautics Limited (HAL): Developing indigenous aircraft like Tejas and helicopters for both domestic and international markets.

Bharat Electronics Limited (BEL): A leader in defense electronics, producing radar systems, communication devices, and missile systems.

Opportunities:

Indigenous Manufacturing: The government's focus on self-reliance through initiatives like "Make in India" is creating opportunities for defense production.

Export Potential: India aims to achieve $5 billion in defense exports by 2025, opening avenues for collaboration with global partners.

Aerospace: Growth in civil aviation and space technology is driving demand for aerospace components and satellite manufacturing.

Global Impact: India's defense exports have grown exponentially, with HAL and BEL emerging as trusted partners for global defense needs.

Why These Sectors Matter

The opportunities in these key sectors underline India's ability to innovate, scale, and address both domestic and global challenges.

Diversified Portfolio: These sectors provide investors with a balanced mix of stability, growth potential, and resilience.

Sustainability and Innovation: Renewable energy and digital transformation are paving the way for a sustainable and technologically advanced future.

Global Relevance: By excelling in pharmaceuticals, IT, and defense, India is cementing its position as a critical player in the global economy.

For global investors, these sectors represent a chance to participate in India's transformative journey, unlocking value in one of the world's most promising markets.

7. Risks and Rewards

India's stock market presents a compelling case for investors with its potential for high returns, driven by a fast-growing economy, diverse sectors, and innovation. However, like any investment landscape, it carries its own set of risks that require careful navigation. Here's a comprehensive exploration of the risks and rewards associated with investing in India's stock market:

Rewards: Unparalleled Growth Potential

India's stock market offers a unique blend of opportunities, thanks to its robust economic fundamentals and expanding sectors.

High Growth Economy: With a GDP growth rate consistently among the highest globally, India offers investors exposure to one of the most dynamic economies. The rising middle class and increasing urbanization are fueling demand across industries such as consumer goods, IT, and healthcare.

Sectoral Diversity: From large-cap stalwarts like Reliance Industries and HDFC Bank to midcap growth stories like LTTS and RateGain, India's market caters to a range of investment strategies. Emerging sectors like renewable energy, fintech, and biotech provide cutting-edge opportunities for high returns.

Favorable Demographics: India's young, tech-savvy population drives consumption, digital transformation, and entrepreneurship, creating a fertile ground for investment.

Global Integration: India's open foreign investment policies, participation in global supply chains, and increasing exports make it a key player in the global economy.

Digital Revolution: The rise of digital trading platforms and financial literacy initiatives has democratized access to the stock market, ensuring greater liquidity and participation.

Risks: Navigating the Challenges

Investing in India also involves inherent risks that must be understood and managed.

Market Volatility:

External Influences: Global economic conditions, such as inflation, recession fears, or geopolitical tensions, can lead to significant market fluctuations.

Domestic Factors: Policy announcements, election outcomes, and macroeconomic indicators (e.g., inflation, fiscal deficit) can impact investor sentiment.

Mitigation Strategy: Diversify investments across sectors and time horizons to cushion against volatility.

Sectoral Shifts:

Rapid Innovation: Sectors like IT and renewable energy are evolving quickly, but traditional industries may face obsolescence due to technological disruption.

Changing Consumer Preferences: Shifts in consumer behavior, such as the preference for sustainable products, can alter the fortunes of certain industries.

Mitigation Strategy: Monitor market trends and invest in companies that demonstrate adaptability and innovation.

Regulatory Changes:

Evolving Policies: India's regulatory environment is dynamic, with frequent changes in FDI rules, taxation, and sector-specific regulations.

Compliance Risks: Non-compliance with local laws and regulations can result in penalties or operational delays.

Mitigation Strategy: Stay informed through legal advisors, trade groups, and government platforms like Invest India.

Currency Fluctuations: For foreign investors, the Indian rupee's volatility against major currencies like the US dollar can affect returns.

Mitigation Strategy: Use hedging tools such as currency futures or options to manage forex risks.

Political and Economic Stability: Political transitions or economic disruptions, such as unexpected fiscal deficits, can impact investor confidence.

Mitigation Strategy: Focus on companies with strong fundamentals and low exposure to government policy changes.

Striking the Balance

Investing in India's stock market requires balancing its high-growth potential with its inherent risks.

Rewards to Embrace: Exceptional growth opportunities in key sectors like IT, renewable energy, and healthcare.

Rising retail participation and innovative trading platforms ensuring liquidity and accessibility.

Risks to Manage: Volatility arising from external and internal factors.

The need for continuous adaptation to evolving regulatory and market environments.

Why India Remains Attractive Despite Risks

India's resilience in overcoming global crises, such as the COVID-19 pandemic and geopolitical challenges, demonstrates its robustness as an investment destination.

Long-Term Vision: India's Vision 2047 and initiatives like the Production Linked Incentive (PLI) scheme underscore its commitment to sustainable growth and innovation.

Strategic Diversification: The diversity of India's stock market—ranging from large caps to midcaps and PSUs—enables investors to build a balanced portfolio that aligns with their risk tolerance and growth objectives.

For investors, the key lies in leveraging India's opportunities while proactively managing its challenges. With the right strategy and insights, India's stock market offers a path to substantial rewards, making it one of the most compelling investment destinations globally.

8. Success Stories

India's dynamic economy and vibrant stock market have produced several success stories that highlight the transformative potential of visionary strategies, innovative solutions, and a deep understanding of local markets. These examples illustrate how companies have disrupted industries, created exponential value for investors, and become benchmarks of growth and resilience.

Reliance Jio: Transforming Telecom and Digital Connectivity

The Story: In 2016, Reliance Jio entered a highly competitive telecom market dominated by established players like Airtel and Vodafone. With a bold strategy of offering free voice calls and affordable data services, Jio revolutionized the sector, making high-speed internet accessible to millions.

Key Success Factors:

Disruptive Pricing: Jio's free introductory offers and low-cost plans forced competitors to lower their tariffs, reshaping the telecom industry.

Digital Ecosystem: Beyond connectivity, Jio developed a digital ecosystem with apps like JioTV, JioCinema, and JioSaavn, integrating entertainment, e-commerce, and financial services.

Market Leadership: Jio's innovative approach rapidly captured a significant market share, reaching over 450 million subscribers by 2024.

Investor Impact: Jio's success boosted the valuation of its parent company, Reliance Industries, making it one of the most valuable companies in India and a favorite among global investors.

TCS: Consistency in Growth and Returns

The Story: As India's largest IT services provider, Tata Consultancy Services (TCS) has consistently delivered value to shareholders through innovation, global expansion, and operational excellence.

Key Success Factors:

Global Presence: TCS serves Fortune 500 companies worldwide, offering solutions in AI, cloud computing, and digital transformation.

Focus on Innovation: Significant investments in R&D have enabled TCS to stay ahead in emerging technologies.

Strong Leadership: TCS has maintained consistent leadership in the IT sector, backed by the Tata Group's ethical business practices.

Investor Impact: TCS has been a consistent performer on the stock market, delivering substantial returns through steady growth and regular dividends.

Maruti Suzuki: Revolutionizing the Automobile Market

The Story: Maruti Suzuki's entry into India's automobile market in the 1980s marked a turning point for the industry. By focusing on affordability and reliability, it became a household name, dominating the market for decades.

Key Success Factors:

Affordable Mobility: Maruti's models like the Maruti 800, Alto, and WagonR provided reliable and fuel-efficient options for the growing middle class.

Strong Dealer Network: A comprehensive dealership and service network ensured accessibility across urban and rural areas.

Adaptation and Innovation: New launches like Brezza and Baleno reflect Maruti's ability to adapt to changing consumer preferences.

Investor Impact: Maruti Suzuki has consistently rewarded investors through capital appreciation and dividends, maintaining a leading market share of over 40%.

Infosys: Elevating India's IT Industry to Global Heights

The Story: Founded in 1981, Infosys began as a small IT services firm and grew into one of the most respected companies globally, driving India's reputation as an IT powerhouse.

Key Success Factors:

Global Delivery Model: Infosys pioneered the offshore outsourcing model, providing cost-effective and high-quality IT services.

Focus on Talent Development: Investments in training and upskilling employees ensured a steady supply of world-class IT professionals.

Client-Centric Approach: Long-term relationships with global clients helped Infosys achieve steady growth.

Investor Impact: Infosys has been a wealth creator for investors, delivering consistent growth and attractive dividends while maintaining a strong balance sheet.

Hindustan Unilever Limited (HUL): A Consumer Goods Titan

The Story: HUL has been instrumental in meeting the needs of India's evolving consumer base, offering a diverse range of products across food, personal care, and household categories.

Key Success Factors:

Rural Penetration: Innovative distribution strategies, like the Shakti program, empowered rural women to sell HUL's products in remote areas.

Product Innovation: Launching affordable SKUs tailored to India's price-sensitive market ensured mass-market appeal.

Brand Loyalty: Iconic brands like Dove, Surf Excel, and Maggi enjoy enduring consumer trust and loyalty.

Investor Impact:

HUL's consistent financial performance and dividend payouts make it a preferred choice for long-term investors.

Adani Green Energy: Pioneering Renewable Energy Growth

The Story: As a leader in renewable energy, Adani Green Energy has positioned itself at the forefront of India's transition to sustainable energy sources.

Key Success Factors:

Mega Solar Projects: Development of large-scale solar and wind power plants aligns with India's ambitious renewable energy goals.

Global Partnerships: Collaborations with international investors and technology providers have bolstered growth.

Visionary Leadership: The Adani Group's strategic focus on sustainability has ensured long-term relevance.

Investor Impact: Adani Green Energy has been a high-growth stock, reflecting investor confidence in India's renewable energy potential.

Lessons from Success Stories

Adaptability and Innovation: Companies that anticipate market trends and adapt their strategies achieve lasting success.

Consumer Focus: Understanding and addressing consumer needs, whether in telecom, IT, or FMCG, drives market leadership.

Strategic Investments: Long-term vision and investment in infrastructure, technology, and talent yield substantial rewards.

These success stories not only highlight India's potential as an investment destination but also offer a blueprint for navigating its diverse and dynamic market. For global investors, they underscore the opportunities that await those who approach India with a blend of vision, strategy, and commitment.

9. The Future of India's Stock Market

India's stock market is poised for unprecedented growth, reflecting the country's evolving economic landscape, technological innovation, and global integration. As the financial ecosystem matures, new opportunities and trends are shaping the future of investing in India. Here's an expanded look at the key factors driving the growth of India's stock market and the trends investors should watch:

Digital Advancements: Revolutionizing Market Operations

Technological innovation is transforming the Indian stock market, making it more efficient, transparent, and accessible.

Blockchain Technology: Blockchain is being integrated into trading systems to enhance security and reduce settlement times. Real-time tracking of transactions ensures greater transparency, minimizing fraud and errors. Exchanges like NSE and BSE are exploring blockchain for smoother clearing and settlement processes.

AI and Big Data Analytics: Artificial Intelligence (AI) is being used for predictive market analysis, algorithmic trading, and personalized investment advice. Big data analytics enables brokers and financial institutions to understand market trends and consumer behavior, optimizing trading strategies.

Digital Platforms for Investors: Apps and platforms like Zerodha, Groww, and Paytm Money have democratized investing, enabling millions to participate in the stock market with user-friendly interfaces and low entry barriers. Features like robo-advisors and automated portfolio management are empowering retail investors with sophisticated tools previously available only to institutions.

Global Integration: Attracting Foreign Investments

India's financial markets are becoming increasingly integrated with the global economy, enhancing their appeal to international investors.

Alignment with Global Standards: India is aligning its regulatory framework with global best practices, enhancing investor confidence. Adopting International Financial Reporting Standards (IFRS) ensures transparency and comparability for foreign portfolio investors (FPIs).

Inclusion in Global Indices: India's increasing weightage in global indices such as MSCI Emerging Markets and FTSE Russell is attracting institutional investments from global fund managers.

Foreign Portfolio Investments (FPI): Simplified FPI registration processes and favorable policies are driving record inflows, particularly into high-growth sectors like IT, banking, and renewable energy.

Global Collaborations: Partnerships with international stock exchanges, such as the NSE's tie-up with the Singapore Exchange (SGX), facilitate seamless trading for foreign investors.

Sectoral Diversification: Exploring New Frontiers

India's stock market is expanding beyond traditional sectors, offering opportunities in emerging industries that reflect the country's innovative spirit and changing priorities.

Fintech Revolution: Fintech companies like Paytm, Policybazaar, and Zomato are redefining financial services and consumer behavior, offering investors exposure to digital transformation. Innovations in digital lending, payment platforms, and neo-banking are creating a robust pipeline of high-growth fintech stocks.

Biotechnology and Healthcare: Companies like Biocon, Dr. Reddy's, and Serum Institute are at the forefront of biotech advancements, capitalizing on global demand for innovative healthcare solutions. The focus on biosimilars, personalized medicine, and vaccine exports presents lucrative opportunities for investors.

Electric Vehicles (EVs): India's transition to electric mobility is driving growth in companies like Tata Motors, Hero Electric, and Ather Energy. The government's push for EV adoption through incentives like FAME (Faster Adoption and Manufacturing of Hybrid and Electric Vehicles) schemes ensures long-term sectoral growth.

Green Technologies: Renewable energy giants like Adani Green Energy and NTPC are leading the charge in solar, wind, and green hydrogen projects, aligning with global sustainability goals.

Retail Participation: Broadening Market Base

Retail investors are becoming a dominant force in India's stock market, reflecting a democratization of financial opportunities.

Rise of Systematic Investment Plans (SIPs): SIP inflows have reached record levels, underlining the growing trend of disciplined, long-term investment among retail participants.

Increased Awareness and Accessibility: Government initiatives, educational programs, and social media influencers are making investing more approachable, particularly for first-time investors.

Regional Penetration: The proliferation of digital trading platforms is enabling individuals from Tier 2 and Tier 3 cities to actively participate in equity markets.

Technological and Regulatory Evolution

Continuous advancements in technology and proactive regulatory measures are ensuring a resilient and future-ready stock market.

Smart Regulations: SEBI's focus on investor protection and market integrity has resulted in stringent disclosure norms and grievance redressal systems. Automation in compliance and reporting processes reduces operational hurdles for companies and ensures market transparency.

Decentralized Trading: Innovations like decentralized finance (DeFi) are being explored to enable secure and efficient trading practices.

Why India's Stock Market Is the Future

The convergence of digital innovation, global integration, and sectoral diversification positions India's stock market as a beacon of growth and resilience. For investors, these trends signify a market that is not only expanding in size but also maturing in sophistication, offering unparalleled opportunities for long-term wealth creation.

India's stock market is more than an economic barometer—it is a reflection of a nation that is rapidly evolving to meet the challenges of the future while creating value for its stakeholders across the globe.

Conclusion

India's stock market has emerged as a compelling destination for investors, embodying the country's rapid economic growth, innovation, and diverse opportunities. For both domestic and international investors, it offers a unique combination of stability through established large-cap companies and exponential growth potential in emerging sectors. With its vibrant mix of traditional industries and cutting-edge technology-driven enterprises, the market reflects the dynamic spirit of the Indian economy.

A Magnet for Growth and Opportunity

India's stock market is more than just a trading platform; it is a cornerstone of the nation's economic development and a gateway to its transformative story.

Stability Meets Growth: Large-cap companies like Reliance Industries, TCS, and HDFC Bank provide a solid foundation, while midcap and small-cap firms offer avenues for high-growth returns.

Sectoral Diversity: From renewable energy and pharmaceuticals to fintech and electric vehicles, India's stock market spans industries that are shaping the future of global commerce.

Resilience: Despite global challenges such as economic downturns and geopolitical uncertainties, India's markets have demonstrated remarkable resilience, underpinned by strong domestic demand and forward-thinking policies.

The Role of Strategic Investment

Success in India's stock market requires more than capital—it demands insight, strategy, and a nuanced understanding of the market landscape.

Leveraging Government Support: Initiatives like the Production Linked Incentive (PLI) schemes, Startup India, and policy reforms create a conducive environment for businesses and investors alike.

Sector-Specific Focus: Identifying and investing in high-potential sectors such as IT, renewable energy, healthcare, and defense ensures alignment with India's growth trajectory.

Retail Participation: The rise in retail investors underscores the democratization of wealth creation in India, adding liquidity and depth to the market.

India: Beyond a Market, a Thriving Ecosystem

India's stock market is not merely a financial arena; it is a reflection of the nation's broader economic aspirations and innovative spirit.

Aspiring to Global Leadership: With initiatives like Vision 2047 and advancements in industries like AI, biotech, and space technology, India is positioning itself as a global economic powerhouse.

Cultural and Economic Synergy: The market captures the unique synergy of India's traditional strengths and modern innovations, creating opportunities that resonate with a wide range of investors.

A Gateway for Transformation: For global leaders, the stock market serves as a gateway to be part of India's transformative journey, enabling participation in its bold steps toward sustainability, inclusivity, and technological leadership.

Promise for Visionaries

For those with the vision to see beyond short-term fluctuations and the resilience to navigate complexities, India's stock market promises substantial rewards.

Wealth Creation: With its vibrant mix of companies and sectors, the market offers investors opportunities for substantial wealth creation across different time horizons.

Economic Participation: Investing in India's stock market is not just about financial gains; it is about being part of a story where economic growth aligns with societal progress and innovation.

Looking Ahead

India's stock market mirrors the aspirations of a country on the rise—a nation that is redefining its place in the global order while staying true to its unique identity. As India continues to innovate and expand, its stock market will remain at the heart of its economic engine, offering unparalleled opportunities for those ready to embrace its potential.

For global investors and leaders, the time to invest in India is now. It is a chance to contribute to and benefit from the remarkable journey of a nation that is shaping the trajectory of the 21st century.

15. Conclusion: Seizing the Magnetic Opportunities in India

India stands at the crossroads of history and opportunity, emerging as a global magnet for investment, innovation, and growth. Its unique blend of economic resilience, dynamic sectors, and visionary policies positions the nation as a transformative force in the 21st century. For investors seeking both stability and growth, India offers an unparalleled landscape of possibilities.

Recap of India's Strengths as an Investment Destination

India's investment magnetism lies in its multifaceted strengths, which have been highlighted throughout this book:

India's Investment Magnetism: A Closer Look at Key Strengths

India's emergence as a global investment destination is built on a foundation of robust economic fundamentals, innovative industries, and forward-thinking policies. Here's a deeper exploration of the strengths that make India a magnet for investors worldwide:

Economic Resilience: A Pillar of Stability

India's economy has demonstrated remarkable resilience, consistently delivering robust GDP growth even in the face of global challenges.

Crisis Response: During the COVID-19 pandemic, India maintained economic stability through timely fiscal and monetary interventions, showcasing its ability to adapt to unpredictable circumstances.

Domestic Demand-Driven Economy: Unlike export-reliant economies, India's growth is largely fueled by its internal demand. This acts as a buffer against global economic slowdowns, ensuring steady performance.

Diverse Economic Base: India's balanced economic structure—comprising agriculture, manufacturing, and services—provides multiple growth avenues and reduces dependency on any single sector.

Dynamic Sectors: Engines of Growth

India's sectoral diversity reflects its ability to innovate and adapt to global trends, making it an ideal investment destination for varied interests.

Information Technology (IT): Companies like TCS, Infosys, and Wipro continue to lead globally in IT services, driving digital transformation worldwide.

Pharmaceuticals and Healthcare: India's role as the "pharmacy of the world" is complemented by its leadership in biotech and medical tourism, offering investors access to global healthcare markets.

Renewable Energy: With ambitious goals like achieving 500 GW of renewable energy capacity by 2030, India is fostering growth in solar, wind, and green hydrogen sectors through companies like Adani Green and Tata Power.

Fintech and Startups: A thriving fintech ecosystem, supported by digital payment platforms like UPI and a vibrant startup culture, is creating new opportunities for investors in cutting-edge industries.

Favorable Demographics: The Power of Youth

India's demographic advantage is a key driver of its economic dynamism and future potential.

Youthful Workforce: With a median age of just 28 years, India's young population contributes to a vibrant labor market and fuels consumer demand across industries.

Tech-Savvy Population: Rising digital literacy and internet penetration empower a generation of tech-driven entrepreneurs and consumers, accelerating the pace of innovation.

Consumption Boom: The burgeoning middle class is reshaping consumption patterns, driving growth in sectors like retail, FMCG, and e-commerce.

Policy Support: Fostering a Pro-Business Environment

India's government has introduced a suite of initiatives to attract investment, simplify operations, and spur economic growth.

Make in India: Encouraging domestic manufacturing and positioning India as a global production hub, this initiative has attracted significant FDI across sectors like electronics, automotive, and defense.

Startup India: Providing funding, tax incentives, and mentorship for startups, this program has fostered a robust innovation ecosystem.

Production Linked Incentive (PLI) Schemes: These schemes offer financial incentives to boost production in key sectors like electronics, pharmaceuticals, and renewable energy, driving industrial growth.

Ease of Doing Business: Reforms in tax structures, regulatory processes, and licensing requirements have enhanced India's ranking in the World Bank's Ease of Doing Business index, bolstering investor confidence.

Global Integration: Strengthening Ties with the World

India's increasing integration into the global financial system enhances its appeal as an investment destination.

Global Financial Standards: Adoption of International Financial Reporting Standards (IFRS) ensures transparency and comparability for foreign investors.

Inclusion in International Indices: India's growing weightage in indices like MSCI and FTSE has attracted institutional investments from global fund managers.

Strategic Collaborations: Bilateral trade agreements and participation in global forums like the G20 highlight India's commitment to international partnerships and economic cooperation.

Innovation Ecosystem: A Hub for Entrepreneurial Growth

India's innovation-driven culture has established it as a global leader in entrepreneurship and technological advancements.

Startup Boom: With over 100 unicorns as of 2024, India is the third-largest startup ecosystem globally. Companies in sectors like fintech, edtech, and healthtech are redefining industry norms.

Robust Financial Markets: Digital trading platforms and increased retail participation have democratized investing, creating a vibrant stock market ecosystem.

Academic-Industry Collaboration: Partnerships between research institutions, industries, and the government are driving breakthroughs in green hydrogen, AI, and space technology.

Why India Stands Out

India's combination of economic resilience, sectoral diversity, youthful demographics, and supportive policies makes it a standout destination for investment. Its capacity to innovate, integrate globally, and adapt to changing dynamics ensures long-term value creation for investors.

India's stock market, dynamic industries, and transformative policies offer a window into the future of global economic leadership. With a foundation built on stability and growth, India continues to magnetize investors seeking to participate in the rise of one of the world's most promising economies.

Encouragement for Investors to Take Action

India is not just an investment destination—it is a transformative journey, a chance to be part of a nation's rise as a global powerhouse. With its unique blend of economic growth, societal progress, and technological innovation, India offers investors an unparalleled opportunity to create value while contributing to a remarkable story of development and inclusion. The momentum is building, and the time to act is now.

1. Identify Key Opportunities

India's vast and diverse economy offers opportunities across multiple sectors, each aligned with global trends and domestic priorities.

Sectors on the Rise: Renewable energy, healthcare, and technology are among the most promising sectors, driven by government initiatives and market demand.

Renewable Energy: Companies like Adani Green Energy and Tata Power are leading India's transition to sustainable energy, creating opportunities for green investments.

Healthcare and Pharmaceuticals: With companies like Sun Pharma and Dr. Reddy's, India remains at the forefront of global healthcare innovation.

Technology and Digital Transformation: Industry leaders like TCS, Infosys, and emerging fintech companies are capitalizing on AI, IoT, and blockchain technologies.

Strong Fundamentals: Focus on companies with sound financial health, innovative business models, and long-term growth strategies that align with India's vision for sustainable and inclusive development.

2. Leverage Local Insights

India's diversity is its strength, but navigating its complex markets requires a nuanced approach. Collaborating with local experts and partners can make the difference between success and missed opportunities.

Local Partnerships: Partnering with Indian businesses and advisors provides critical insights into regulatory landscapes, consumer behavior, and regional opportunities. This collaboration helps investors navigate cultural nuances and operational challenges.

Regional Dynamics: India's markets vary significantly across regions, with Tier 2 and Tier 3 cities offering untapped potential. Understanding regional consumption patterns and economic drivers ensures tailored strategies that resonate with local populations.

Consumer Behavior: India's young, tech-savvy population is shaping new trends in consumption and digital adoption. Investors who grasp these dynamics can align their offerings to meet evolving demands effectively.

3. Embrace Long-Term Vision

India's growth story is a marathon, not a sprint. Investors who take a long-term perspective are better positioned to reap substantial rewards as the nation continues to expand and evolve.

Patience Pays: India's markets can experience short-term volatility due to global economic fluctuations or policy changes. However, the country's robust fundamentals and diverse economy ensure long-term resilience.

Infrastructure and Innovation: Long-term investments in infrastructure projects, such as industrial corridors, smart cities, and digital connectivity, promise consistent returns while contributing to India's development goals.

Entrepreneurial Ventures: India's vibrant startup ecosystem offers high-growth opportunities in fintech, e-commerce, and medtech, making it an ideal landscape for venture capital and private equity investments.

4. Contribute to India's Growth

Investing in India is more than a financial decision—it is a meaningful contribution to a nation's rise to global prominence.

Supporting Innovation: Your investments fuel innovation in key areas like renewable energy, healthcare, and technology, enabling solutions that address global challenges.

Job Creation: Investments in sectors like manufacturing, IT, and services generate employment opportunities, empowering India's workforce and uplifting communities.

Sustainable Development: By aligning investments with India's sustainability goals, such as renewable energy adoption and green infrastructure, you support initiatives that ensure long-term environmental and economic stability.

A Call to Action

India's investment landscape is ripe with possibilities, and the momentum of its economic transformation is undeniable. By seizing the opportunities available today, investors can align themselves with a nation poised to redefine the future of global commerce and innovation.

Be a Partner in Progress: Investing in India allows you to participate in a story of growth, resilience, and transformation. It's a chance to contribute to a nation's ambitious journey while reaping financial rewards.

Unlock Untapped Potential: India's diverse markets, innovative industries, and youthful workforce create a fertile ground for investors with vision and strategic intent.

Shape the Future: Your investment not only strengthens your portfolio but also shapes India's trajectory as a leader in global innovation and sustainable development.

India is calling on investors with the foresight to see its potential, the strategy to navigate its complexities, and the resilience to stay the course. The time to act is now—seize the magnetic opportunities that India offers and be part of a transformative journey that defines the 21st century.

India: The Magnet of Possibilities

India stands as a beacon of opportunity, drawing attention not only for its vibrant markets and dynamic sectors but also for its resilient people, groundbreaking innovations, and visionary goals. It is a land where tradition meets modernity, and ambition fuels progress. For investors, entrepreneurs, and global leaders, India represents more than an economic destination—it is a transformative journey into a future shaped by possibilities.

A Vibrant Ecosystem of Growth and Innovation

India's investment magnetism transcends conventional boundaries, reflecting its unique ability to adapt, innovate, and lead.

The Human Capital Advantage: With one of the youngest populations in the world, India is powered by a demographic dividend that drives entrepreneurship, technological adoption, and economic dynamism.

Its skilled and tech-savvy workforce continues to make strides in industries like IT, healthcare, and renewable energy, creating value for global markets.

Innovation at Its Core: India's robust startup ecosystem, supported by government initiatives and private investments, has produced over 100 unicorns as of 2024, showcasing its capacity for innovation.

Breakthroughs in AI, blockchain, and green technologies are not just addressing domestic challenges but contributing to global advancements.

A Global Vision: India's Vision 2047 outlines its ambitious goals to emerge as a global economic powerhouse, emphasizing sustainability, inclusivity, and technological leadership.

This vision aligns with global priorities, ensuring that India's growth story resonates across borders and contributes to shaping the global economic order.

Seizing the Vast Opportunities

The opportunities in India span across sectors and geographies, reflecting the diversity and depth of its economy.

Dynamic Markets: From large-cap leaders like Reliance Industries and TCS to emerging midcap stars and government enterprises, India's stock market offers investment avenues for every profile.

The rise of retail participation and the democratization of investing through digital platforms highlight India's financial inclusivity and potential for sustained growth.

Emerging Sectors: High-growth industries like fintech, electric vehicles, and biotech present unprecedented opportunities for those ready to invest in innovation and disruption.

Renewable energy giants and sustainable infrastructure projects are paving the way for long-term, impactful investments.

Regional Expansion: The rise of Tier 2 and Tier 3 cities as new growth hubs showcases India's untapped potential beyond its metropolitan centers.

Investments in infrastructure and connectivity are opening new frontiers, creating opportunities for local and global players alike.

The Time to Act Is Now

India's magnetic pull is not just about the opportunities of today—it is about the promise of tomorrow.

Defining the Future: As a nation that blends resilience with innovation, India is poised to redefine the global economic order in the coming decades.

By investing in India, you align yourself with a country that is shaping the trajectory of industries, technologies, and societal progress.

Real and Tangible Rewards: The combination of economic stability, high-growth potential, and sectoral diversity ensures meaningful returns for those with vision and strategy.

Beyond financial gains, investing in India offers the fulfillment of contributing to a transformative journey that impacts billions of lives.

A Call to Embrace the Magnetism

India is not just defining its own future—it is influencing the trajectory of the world. The nation's magnetic pull is a testament to its boundless energy, creativity, and drive to excel.

For global leaders and investors, India is a gateway to unparalleled opportunities. By embracing this vibrant ecosystem, you join a movement that is shaping the future of global innovation, sustainability, and economic progress.

The possibilities in India are vast, the potential is limitless, and the rewards are real. Let India's magnetic pull guide your next move. It is a decision that promises not just growth but a role in a story of transformation and progress—a story that defines the 21st century.

Appendices

To further support investors in navigating India's dynamic investment landscape, this section provides essential resources, including investment-friendly locations, key government contacts, and a glossary of terms relevant to India's markets.

Appendix A

List of Investment-Friendly States and Cities

India's diversity extends to its economic hubs, each offering unique advantages for investors:

States Leading the Way

Maharashtra: Home to Mumbai, the financial capital of India, with a strong industrial and services base.

Karnataka: A hub for IT, biotech, and aerospace, anchored by Bengaluru.

Tamil Nadu: Renowned for automotive and manufacturing excellence, including Chennai's industrial corridors.

Gujarat: Known for business-friendly policies, robust infrastructure, and strong manufacturing sectors.

Uttar Pradesh: Emerging as a leader in renewable energy and electronics manufacturing.

Rajasthan: Promising growth in renewable energy and tourism industries.

Cities to Watch

Mumbai: India's financial nerve center with opportunities in banking, fintech, and media.

Bengaluru: The Silicon Valley of India, a leader in tech startups and innovation.

Hyderabad: Growing as a hub for biotech, pharmaceuticals, and IT.

Chennai: Strong in manufacturing, especially in automotive and electronics.

Pune: A hub for education, IT, and automotive industries.

Ahmedabad: Rapidly growing in textiles, pharma, and renewable energy.

Appendix B

Key Government Contacts and Schemes

Government Bodies:

Invest India: The national investment promotion agency offering comprehensive support to investors.

DPIIT (Department for Promotion of Industry and Internal Trade): Guides investors on policies and provides sector-specific information.

State Investment Boards: Each state has dedicated investment promotion boards, such as the Maharashtra Industrial Development Corporation (MIDC) and Karnataka Udyog Mitra.

Key Schemes for Investors:

Make in India: Encourages domestic manufacturing with incentives and streamlined processes.

Production Linked Incentive (PLI) Schemes: Offers financial benefits across sectors like electronics, pharmaceuticals, and solar modules.

Startup India: Provides funding, tax benefits, and mentorship for entrepreneurs.

Digital India: Promotes digital transformation and innovation across industries.

National Infrastructure Pipeline (NIP): A $1.5 trillion investment plan for infrastructure projects by 2025.

Single Window Clearance System: Simplifies the process of obtaining necessary licenses and permits for businesses.

Appendix C
Glossary of Terms for Investors

FDI (Foreign Direct Investment): Investment from foreign entities directly into Indian businesses, often with ownership control.

FPI (Foreign Portfolio Investment): Investment by foreign individuals or entities in Indian financial assets like stocks and bonds.

Nifty50: A benchmark index on the NSE, representing the top 50 companies by market capitalization.

BSE Sensex: A benchmark index on the BSE, representing 30 well-established companies across sectors.

SIP (Systematic Investment Plan): A disciplined approach to investing in mutual funds through regular, fixed contributions.

GST (Goods and Services Tax): A unified tax structure replacing multiple indirect taxes, streamlining business operations.

PLI (Production Linked Incentive): A government scheme incentivizing companies for incremental production in key sectors.

IPO (Initial Public Offering): The process by which a company offers its shares to the public for the first time.

Make in India: A government initiative aimed at boosting manufacturing and making India a global production hub.

ATMs (Alternate Trading Mechanisms): Trading systems like block deals and bulk trades outside the regular market.

These appendices are designed to provide quick access to vital information, ensuring investors have the tools they need to make informed decisions and capitalize on India's dynamic opportunities.

Resources

This section provides a curated list of recommended readings, reports, and market analyses to help investors gain deeper insights into India's investment landscape and emerging opportunities.

Recommended Readings

Books:

India: The Emerging Giant by Arvind Panagariya – An in-depth analysis of India's economic transformation.

The Billionaire Raj by James Crabtree – Explores India's economic rise through the lens of its wealthiest business leaders.

India Unbound by Gurcharan Das – A comprehensive narrative on India's journey from socialism to economic liberalization.

Globalization and Its Discontents by Joseph E. Stiglitz – Offers a global perspective on economic challenges and opportunities, relevant to India's evolving role.

Industry-Specific Reads:

The Indian Startup Ecosystem: Drivers, Challenges, and Future – A detailed look at India's vibrant entrepreneurial landscape.

Renewable Energy in India: Trends and Opportunities – Highlights the growth and potential in India's sustainable energy sector.

Reports and Market Analyses

Government Publications:

Economic Survey of India: Published annually, this document provides a comprehensive overview of India's economic performance and policy initiatives.

India Investment Grid: A government-backed resource detailing investment opportunities across sectors and states.

Institutional Reports:

World Bank's Ease of Doing Business Report: Insights into India's reforms and rankings.

McKinsey & Company's India Reports: Industry-specific analyses and growth projections.

KPMG India Economic Survey: Highlights emerging trends and investment strategies.

Sectoral Insights:

NASSCOM Reports: In-depth data on India's IT and software services sector.

FICCI (Federation of Indian Chambers of Commerce and Industry) White Papers: Covering industries like healthcare, fintech, and retail.

Renewable Energy Country Attractiveness Index (RECAI) by EY: Evaluates India's potential in renewable energy investments.

Market Analysis Platforms

Stock Market Platforms:

NSE India: Offers market trends, stock indices, and corporate filings.

BSE India: Provides historical data, IPO updates, and market analytics.

Investment Research Portals:

Morningstar India: Detailed analysis of mutual funds, stocks, and ETFs.

CRISIL Reports: Credit ratings and sectoral research for informed decision-making.

CMIE (Centre for Monitoring Indian Economy): Macroeconomic data and insights.

Global Perspectives:

World Economic Forum (WEF) Reports on India: Analyzes India's role in the global economy.

IMF (International Monetary Fund) Country Reports: Updates on India's economic outlook.

Online Resources and Databases

Government Portals:

Invest India Website: A one-stop platform for investment guidance.

Startup India Portal: Resources for entrepreneurs and investors in India's startup ecosystem.

Trade and Industry Platforms:

India Brand Equity Foundation (IBEF): Comprehensive data on industries, exports, and economic initiatives.

Export-Import Bank of India (EXIM Bank): Sector-specific export trends and reports.

Media and Market Watch:

The Economic Times: Regular updates on business and financial news.

Mint: Focused on stock markets, policies, and investments.

BloombergQuint: Global and domestic market trends with expert analysis.

This resources section equips investors with the knowledge and tools to make informed decisions, navigate India's opportunities, and align their strategies with the country's transformative growth story.

Acknowledgments

This book is the culmination of insights, research, and experiences gathered from diverse sources and inspiring individuals who have shaped its journey. It would not have been possible without the guidance, support, and contributions of several people and institutions.

First and foremost, I am deeply grateful to **my family** for their unwavering encouragement and patience throughout this project. Their belief in my vision has been my constant source of strength.

A heartfelt thanks to the **readers, researchers, and industry experts** who shared their perspectives, experiences, and valuable insights, enriching the content and ensuring its relevance to today's global investment landscape. Your expertise has helped shape this book into a comprehensive guide.

I owe immense gratitude to the **Indian government bodies, trade organizations, and industry associations** whose reports, data, and initiatives have provided the foundation for much of the content. The visionary reforms and programs implemented by institutions like **Invest India, DPIIT, and NASSCOM** have been central to this narrative.

A special thanks to the **business leaders, entrepreneurs, and investors** whose real-world stories have inspired many of the case studies included in this book. Your successes and challenges offer invaluable lessons for anyone considering investing in India.

To the **publishers and editorial team**, thank you for your meticulous work, attention to detail, and dedication to ensuring that this book meets the highest standards of quality and accessibility.

Lastly, my gratitude goes to **India itself**—its people, its resilience, and its boundless potential. This nation's transformative journey continues to inspire and redefine what is possible on the global stage.

This book is dedicated to all those who believe in India's promise and seek to be a part of its remarkable story. Thank you for being part of this journey and for your interest in exploring the magnetic opportunities that India offers.

Sincerely,

Sandeep Chavan

About the Author

Sandeep Chavan is a seasoned professional with decades of experience in engineering, education, and thought leadership. With a deep understanding of India's economic landscape and a passion for fostering global collaboration, the author brings a unique perspective to the dynamic world of investments and development. This book is a reflection of his commitment to empowering investors, entrepreneurs, and policymakers with actionable insights into India's transformative journey.

An industrial engineer turned educator, **Sandeep Chavan** has worked extensively across industries, gaining firsthand experience of India's evolving business environment. Over the years, he has taught and mentored countless students, shaping the next generation of leaders in science, technology, and economics.

With a flair for simplifying complex concepts, **Sandeep Chavan** combines meticulous research with practical knowledge to create a compelling narrative about India's potential as a global investment magnet. The author's work highlights the intersection of innovation, policy, and market opportunities, making it accessible to readers across geographies and industries.

Beyond this book, **Sandeep Chavan** has been an advocate for sustainable growth, financial literacy, and bridging gaps between global investors and India's burgeoning economy. His passion for India's development resonates in the pages of this book, making it a valuable resource for anyone looking to understand and engage with one of the world's most promising economies.

Don't miss out!

Visit the website below and you can sign up to receive emails whenever SANDEEP CHAVAN publishes a new book. There's no charge and no obligation.

https://books2read.com/r/B-A-EPGPC-GJMJF

Connecting independent readers to independent writers.

Did you love *India: The Investment Magnet*? Then you should read *The Triangular Dynamics*[1] by SANDEEP CHAVAN!

[2]

In an era defined by geopolitical complexities and shifting global power dynamics, The Triangular Dynamics: India between China and USA delves into the intricate relationships shaping the 21st-century world order. Written by Sandeep Chavan, this insightful book explores India's pivotal role as a mediator, balancer, and emerging global leader amidst the superpower rivalry between China and the United States.The book examines how India navigates its relationships with two of the most influential nations in the world. By analyzing India's strategic autonomy, diplomatic engagements, and economic strategies, Chavan sheds light on the country's ability to balance its partnerships with the U.S. and China while advancing its own national interests. This balancing act is not merely a survival tactic but a reflection of India's growing stature in global geopolitics.Drawing on a comprehensive analysis of trade, technology, and diplomacy, The Triangular Dynamics

1. https://books2read.com/u/47qPpq

2. https://books2read.com/u/47qPpq

highlights India's initiatives in reshaping global supply chains, fostering innovation, and championing sustainability. From the Production-Linked Incentive (PLI) schemes to the International Solar Alliance, the book showcases India's efforts to redefine its economic and environmental responsibilities on the global stage.Chavan also explores India's leadership in multilateral platforms like BRICS, the Quad, and the G20, positioning it as a voice for the Global South. The book discusses India's role in addressing critical issues such as climate change, digital governance, and public health, emphasizing its ability to act as a bridge between developed and developing nations.With a focus on India's strategic location, rich cultural legacy, and ambitious vision for 2030, The Triangular Dynamics outlines a roadmap for the nation to emerge as a key player in a multipolar world. It underscores the importance of resilience, innovation, and inclusive growth in shaping a more equitable and harmonious global order.Ideal for readers of international relations, political science, and global economics, this book provides a balanced perspective on the challenges and opportunities within the U.S.-China-India triangle. The Triangular Dynamics: India between China and USA is a thought-provoking exploration of the strategies and values that will shape India's role in an interconnected and competitive world.

Read more at www.gyrusvision.com.

Also by SANDEEP CHAVAN

It's Not AI, It's AHI - Amplified Human Intelligence
The Decision Paradox
The Four Sapiens
Malicious Script of Indian Polity
The IIT Legacy & Global Impact
The IIT Legacy & Global Impact
You are just a Version of Your Original
Win the Game You Didn't Choose
Always Keep Your Bags Packed
Reveal to Shield - Learn the Game of Facades
Engage Beyond Elections
Culture, Identity & Change: The Evolution of Indian Society
The Triangular Dynamics
Never Trust Without Doubt
If You Can't Change the Country, Leave the Country
Live Fearless with Fear
India: The Investment Magnet

Watch for more at www.gyrusvision.com.

www.ingramcontent.com/pod-product-compliance
Lightning Source LLC
LaVergne TN
LVHW052310200926
848481LV00002B/522
* 9 7 9 8 2 3 0 4 4 0 5 3 6 *